NORTH SEA IMPACT

Off-shore Oil and the British Economy

NORTH SEA IMPACT
Off-shore Oil and the British Economy

Adrian Hamilton

Introduction
by
Professor Colin Robinson
University of Surrey

International Institute
for Economic Research

First published in March, 1978

Designed and produced by Good Relations Design Ltd.

Printed in Great Britain by Goron Pro-Print Company Limited

ISBN 0 906215 00 5

About the Author

Adrian Hamilton, Industrial Editor of the *Observer* newspaper, has worked in journalism in the U.S. and U.K. since graduating from Oxford with a degree in modern history in 1965. He has been involved in reporting North Sea developments since the first oil discovery off the Norwegian coast and was for six years the *Financial Times* specialist writer on oil and energy matters. He is the author of the *Infamous Essay on Woman,* (1971) a study of John Wilkes, and co-author with Christopher Tugendhat of *Oil, the Biggest Business* (1975).

Acknowledgements

In writing this study, and in my time of reporting the North Sea which went before, the list of colleagues, contacts and friends who have helped is far too long to enumerate. A journalist is essentially a leach of others' words and a plagiariser of others' opinions and I have been singularly fortunate in the kindness and helpfulness of a wide range of those involved in or studying the North Sea development.

But I would like to especially thank Ray Richardson of the LSE, William Keegan of the *Observer* and Sam Brittan of the *Financial Times* for patiently and always generously sharing their wisdom and attempting to drum, however fruitlessly, some economic sense into me; Sir Goıdon Newton for setting me off on the track, Miles Bowen of Shell, Q. Morris, Mike Unstead, Frank Howitt and Mat Huber of BP, J. L. Daniand of Total Oil Marine, Angus Beckett of William Press, Bob MacAlister of Occidental, Martin Lovegrove of Wood Mackenzie, Tony Fox of Incentrol, George Williams of UKOA, Roger Pope of the Energy Department and the many, many people in industry, government and elsewhere who have so patiently explained what it is all about; and, not least my wife, who has always encouraged me to stretch further and organise better.

The three maps at the end of the book are reproduced with the kind permission of the Controller of Her Majesty's Stationery Office. The cross sections of the Brent Field in Chapter 4 are from a paper by Miles Bowen to the Institute of Petroleum Conference, November 1974, and are reproduced with the kind permission of the Institute and Shell U.K. Exploration and Production.

Adrian Hamilton

Contents

Introduction

by Professor Colin Robinson

The discovery of natural gas and oil in the British sector of the North Sea could hardly have been better timed. After the gas finds of the mid-1960s, on the basis of which the gas distribution industry was transformed, came a series of substantial oil finds in the early 1970s at about the time of the massive OPEC oil price increases. Alone among the larger West European nations, Britain's is now on the verge of self-sufficiency in oil and could become a significant net oil exporter in the early 1980s. Mr. Hamilton's book is also well timed. As a journalist whose task it was to follow North Sea affairs, he is in a good position to provide enlightenment on how government and company policies developed and to comment on the wisdom of those policies. At a time when there is so much ill-informed discussion of the supposed massive benefits of North Sea oil and a growing expectation is developing among the populace of large hand-outs, Mr. Hamilton's historical perspective gives us an opportunity to consider how successful have been our past efforts at exploiting the area.

There is much to admire in the technological and managerial expertise which the producing companies have used to conquer the novel problems posed by the North Sea: it is indeed remarkable that by 1977—only about seven years after the first major oil find in the British sector—offshore oil output should be equivalent to almost half the country's oil consumption. Governments also deserve credit for creating conditions in which rapid exploitation could proceed.

However, Mr. Hamilton's description of the history of North Sea development calls to mind certain less happy features of the past and some of the dangers to which we may be subject in the future. Above all, it allows one to take an overall view of the evolution of Government oil and gas policy, observing how it has reached its present state.

In the early days, government involvement in North Sea development was relatively limited. Governments began in the early 1960s by virtually giving away exploration and production licences for the southern North Sea basin: licences were awarded by "administrative discretion". Subsequently, as realisation dawned that the area contained a number of sizeable gas fields and that foreign-owned companies might make "excessive" profits, the Government of the day (1966-68) hastened to strengthen the monopsony position of the Gas Council and Area Boards (now the British Gas Corporation) so as to force a low price on to the companies. This somewhat clumsy attempt to collect natural resource "rent" appears only to have transferred the surplus from North Sea gas production to the Gas Corporation from the oil companies—a procedure for which there is no support in economic theory. At this stage, however, there was little or no control over the rate at which producing companies chose to exploit their finds: the effective constraint on the expansion of output was the Gas Corporation's ability to absorb natural gas into its system.

As time passed, a story unfolded which—although it has its parallel in many countries—is no better for that. It was apparently decided in political and civil service circles (which, as Mr. Hamilton points out, have never encouraged public debate on North Sea affairs) that more control over the North Sea would be desirable. The issue of North Sea licences became increasingly a matter of favouring the interests of British companies and especially British nationalised industries. A limited licence auction was held in 1971 but it was evidently decided that competitive bidding did not give enough control to the administrators. Consequently, when oil was discovered in the early 1970s, the authorities again became alarmed at the prospect of what they deemed to be excessive profits. Since there was no State monopsonist for oil, as there was for natural gas, the rather complicated Petroleum Revenue Tax was devised as an attempt to collect the rent from oil.

Other moves towards greater State control were also in motion. By the mid-1970s both the major political parties had reached the conclusion that some means of regulating North Sea output would be desirable, although the precise method of control was the subject of dispute. The mechanism of detailed regulation now exists in the Labour Government's Petroleum and Submarine Pipelines Act, supplemented by the Energy Act and other powers of government. The present Government is apparently also attempting to ensure that no more than one-third of North Sea crude oil is exported.

No doubt all these controlling devices have been instituted from the best of motives and it may be that some short term benefits (in terms of votes) will accrue to politicians who claim to be able to direct the future development of the North Sea. But in the end efficient central control depends on the ability of our rulers to see into the future (both to determine what would happen if policies were unchanged and to forecast the effects of given changes) and to select the policies which are needed to achieve that elusive concept—the "national interest". One also has to assume that government can not only see the national interest but will pursue it; that is, it can be relied upon to act benevolently towards the rest of society rather than in its own interest.

In his final chapter Mr. Hamilton raises a number of questions which relate to such matters. As he says, historical evidence suggests that people are very much worse at making predictions than they realise. Consequently, some of the conventional assumptions on which energy policy is now being planned—such as belief in an energy gap—are highly questionable and could lead to very large errors. In order to retain the flexibility which is one of the prime requirements in dealing with future uncertainty, a reasonable degree of humility is essential both about one's ability to forecast and about the likely effectiveness of tinkering with the system. It is to be regretted that pressures of self-interest among politicians and civil servants seem to be leading towards ever tighter central control, without heed for the dangers of inflexibility. Mr. Hamilton's review of the history of North Sea exploration ought to make those concerned with policy-making pause to consider the dangers of the road along which they are now leading us.

Colin Robinson

University of Surrey, Guildford, March, 1978.

1 The Gas Revolution

The North Sea has tended to go down in the public mind as the great surprise of the decade—a sudden development which occurred against all the predictions of the oil companies, all the expectations of industry and the knowledge of the Government.

In a sense this is true, at least of the oil discoveries. There were few, even as late as ten years ago, who thought that oil would be discovered off the U.K. shore, still fewer who believed it would be discovered in commercial quantities. Once the oil was discovered, both the speed at which the major finds were recorded and the oil companies went ahead, was quite extraordinary by comparison with anywhere else in the world.

But to subscribe to the image of the "great surprise", is to forget that exploration in the U.K. North Sea started, not in 1970, but six years before, and that for the most of the sixties, the U.K. enjoyed a gas development phase which was not only unique in the North Sea but which also proved a dress rehearsal, in many ways, for what was to occur with oil. The gas development was greeted with the same kind of euphoria as that which greeted the more recent oil developments. The finds made were sizeable by world standards. Their production brought a profound change to the country's fuel supply and consumption patterns. But their output made surprisingly little difference to the British economy as a whole, nor did this development encourage the development of a major new British industry to serve the off-shore search.

When the first off-shore exploration drilling started in December 1964, it was very much with high hopes that large gas finds might be made in the U.K. sector of the North Sea. That drilling and licence allocation had not been made before then, was less a matter of geological doubt or the lack of technical capability in the industry, to drill in the sea, than the lack of the right combination of exploration expectation, technology and legal framework.

All these factors had been present for some time since the Second World War. On the assumption that off-shore prospects were likely to be an extension of on-shore geology, then it could have been pointed out that oil and gas had been found and produced on both sides of the North Sea, in England, Scotland, the Netherlands and Germany more than 20 years previously. An on-shore gas find of considerable interest had been made at Eskdale in Yorkshire in 1937, following the passing of the Petroleum Production Act, 1934, (which first laid down the essential legal framework under which ownership of all mineral oils was vested in the Crown), which then gave companies the licence to explore and produce it. Other gas finds were made near Edinburgh and, after the Second World War, were connected up with local coal-based gas plants to boost local supplies both in Whitby (by 1960) and in south-east Scotland.

The late thirties had also seen the discovery of a significant, though relatively small, oil field at Eakring near Nottingham, followed by a number of other finds in the Midlands area, joined by others in Lincolnshire (Gainsborough) and Dorset (Kimmeridge) in the 1950s. By the early sixties, these finds were, together, producing around 1,500 barrels per day.

This was less than 2 per cent of U.K. oil requirements at the time, but it was sufficient to encourage the geologists of some of the major oil companies to further exploration in the country. The question was less whether oil or gas might be found off-shore than whether, in view of the experience on-shore, it would be found in sufficient quantities to justify the immense additional cost of off-shore production.

In the meantime, both the technology and the legal framework; for off-shore exploration had been developing steadily, first, as companies simply extended facilities from the shore line out into the water in Lake Maracaibo in Venezuela, in the Gulf of Mexico, and in the Persian Gulf, and in the Trucial states; then, as companies became more ambitious, they developed the use of mobile drilling ships or barges to search off-shore, independently of the land.

By the late 1950s, the technology existed both to explore for and produce oil and gas in up to around 100 feet of water, at least in calm water. And there had been a steady progression of bilateral arrangements—pressured largely by the desires of the non-oil producing Middle East states to ascertain their oil resources in the Gulf—and to divide the seabed beyond the traditional three-mile territorial limits. By 1951, more than 42 claims to the Continental Shelf seabed rights had been made around the world, including President Truman's 1945 declaration of U.S. intentions to the seabed around the coast-line and most of the states in the Gulf of Mexico and an early agreement by Britain to divide the sea area of the Gulf of Paria between Trinidad and Venezuela.

What brought these various developments together to promote the North Sea search, was a series of crucial events at the end of the 1950s; the most significant of which was simply need.

The post-war economic resurgence of the major industrialised nations of Europe and Japan and the growth of the U.S. economy was fuelled very largely by oil (and gas in the U.S.), which, during the 1950s, everywhere eroded the predominant place of coal in the consumers' energy patterns, more than doubling its share of Western European primary energy consumption to over a third within the space of a decade.

This great demand for oil was fed continuously by the growth of Middle East production. In one sense, the dramatic expansion of the Middle East could be said to have undermined the economic need to find new sources of oil in high cost areas such as the European off-shore. Certainly it curbed the enthusiasm of the major oil companies for exploring new areas. But the Middle East was also largely in the hands of the major oil companies. Furthermore the growing U.S. market for cheap imports encouraged a number of smaller American oil companies to reach out into the Eastern hemisphere for supplies of their own.

From the point of view of governments, as well, the political problems associated with this dependence on Middle East supplies had been brought home forcefully both by the Iranian oil nationalisation in 1951, which broke the BP near-monopoly of production there, and the Suez venture of 1957, which drove home the limits of traditional British influence over the area. And, for Britain, the position was made even more uncomfortable, in economic terms; by the heavy cost of oil imports on a weakening balance of payments picture (its oil deficit on the balance of payments more than doubled from £181m. in 1950 to £375m. in 1960 in current prices); by the social problems of a contracting coal industry, which was leaving the country with higher energy costs than European competitors using cheap imported oil; and by the serious competitive problems facing the traditionally coal-based gas industry, which was itself turning to oil-based manufacturing processes and imports to maintain its position.

The second factor promoting development, was the achievement of an agreed international framework for dividing the seabed beyond the three mile territorial limits under the 1958 Geneva Convention. The Convention was held under the steady pressure of countries claiming the Continental Shelf rights to oil and minerals and of the degree of conflict arising in gulf areas where these claims were overlapping. Under the Convention, (ratified by the U.K. in 1964 and by most of the other European countries at the same period), nations could claim the rights to exploit the natural resources on their Contingent Continental Shelves—defined as stretching to the 200-metre depth contour or beyond, as far as natural resources could be exploited. In case of dispute, the Convention laid down that the "boundary shall be determined by application of the principle of equidistance from the nearest points of the baselines from which the breadth of the territorial sea of each State is measured".

In the case of the U.K., the shape of the eastern coastline gives it certain advantages, particularly in the southern part, and the division is not too difficult. Where the coastline is concave, as in Denmark, Germany and Holland, the problem is more difficult and, in the event, led to an international court action on the part of Germany, after the original licences for all countries had been awarded (the case ended in Germany's favour in 1970 after three years of consideration and both its neighbours had to give up territory to her). A problem also arises as to the question of whether islands, such as the Scillies, are regarded as part of the mainland or not and whether uninhabited islands such as Rockall can be used for claims. This in turn, has led to a dispute between Britain, Ireland, France and Greenland, over division of territory to the west of the U.K., which, while finally agreed for the Western Approaches, still remains to be resolved to the north around Rockall.[1]

Most intriguingly, it has led to a recurring accusation that the U.K. could have demanded far more of Norwegian territory than it did when the two countries agreed on their boundary south of the 62nd line of latitude in 1965. The reason has been the deep

[1] The 1977 arbitration decision over the Western Approaches and the Channel Islands, following a 13-year dispute between France and Britain, gave no clear hint as to how the other decisions may go. Instead it simply gave Britain a "half" right to claim the Scillies as part of the mainland (effectively dividing the rival claims down the middle) and gave a 12-mile limit to the Channel Islands. This still leaves open the dispute between Ireland and Britain over the division of the Western Approaches off the south of Ireland and between Ireland, Denmark and Britain over the area around Rockall (where there is the added complication that it is uninhabited and therefore of debatable status in the division of the Continental Shelves).

trench which skirts the Norwegian coast close to the shore not far from the coastline itself and which is well over 200 metres in depth for much of its length. One argument has been that, under the Geneva Convention definition of water depths (out to 200 metres), Norway should have had only the territory up to the trench, leaving Britain with almost all the northern North Sea basin, including the territory on which the Ekofisk, Frigg, Statfjord and other major finds have since been made.

Britain did not claim it because, at the time (in 1964-1965), she was in a hurry to get moving, doubted her final recourse in law and did not feel she could afford the delays involved. Whether she might have compromised on more territory than she got (the Norwegians themselves were surprised by the speed and helpfulness with which the U.K. authorities approached the negotiation) is, no doubt, an arguable point. But the Norwegians would have almost certainly claimed—with a good deal of justice on their side—that the area between the two countries was a continuous shelf and that the trench was not a limit to the Shelf in the true sense, but merely a subsidence of the old basement rock, rather than a geologically justified distinction between shelf and ocean floor. Given what occurred in the legal case pursued by Germany, it is hard to avoid the feeling that Britain would not have got away with it and that substantial delays would have occurred (it took around five years for the German case to be settled). Nor, at the time, was there any feeling that the prospects in the area were good enough to justify a prolonged row.

The most important spur to North Sea development however, occurred on the exploration front when the Shell-Esso partnership (NAM), working on land in the Netherlands, announced a gas strike of enormous potential magnitude in Groningen in northern Holland in 1954. The find—itself the product of thirteen years drilling effort and more than 200 wells—was of immense significance. It proved the one point that really excites the exploration industry—that major reserves could be found in the area sufficient to justify high-cost development. Moreover, they seemed sufficient to create a natural gas-based market on the American lines which could replace Europe's previous reliance on expensive gas manufactured out of coal or oil.

The Groningen find also proved a fascinating geological "play", in that the gas was found in Rottligiendes sands deposited in Permian times and overlaying coal measures from which the gas had originally come. The combination of coal, or carboniferous source rocks with overlying sands, forming the reservoir rock, and capped by evaporated salt layers, making up the impermeable seal on the reservoirs, was reminiscent of Middle East fields. And the same conditions were thought, on the basis of the on-shore evidence in England and at the Eskdale on-shore field in Yorkshire, to extend right across the sea between Holland and the U.K. In particular, the fact that the gas seemed to come from the coal measures, a fresh-water deposit, rather than the marine sediments which form the source of most of the world's oil and gas, suggested that the gas province might be an extensive one, provided that the right "traps" existed. It was naturally thought that, from the on-shore evidence, prospects in Dutch waters were better than on the western side, where on-shore evidence suggested much patchier presence of potential reservoirs, but a series of seismic surveys carried out by groups of companies in U.K. waters in the early 1960s did nothing to discourage British prospects.

It was against this background of international agreement for territorial division, exploration enthusiasm after Groningen, the prospect of gas rather than oil as the main target and the overwhelming urgency of British demand for gas or oil, that the Government finally decided to offer blocks under a specially-devised licensing system early in 1964.

It is not yet fully clear why the Government settled on the discretionary licensing system, under which licences were awarded on the basis of factors such as the importance of the company in the U.K. economy, the financial strength of the applicant and the number of wells it was prepared to drill, rather than any cash offer or profit-sharing with the Government. Alternative systems were considered, including an auction system on the basis of cash bids or bonuses on production (as practised in North America) and the profit-sharing schemes then being negotiated on the new concession in the Gulf. The idea of giving most of the territory to BP was also considered. But, in the end, all were rejected for this unusual home-grown system of discretionary licensing.[2]

Part of the reason must lie in the personality and thinking of the civil servant most directly concerned, Mr. Angus Beckett.[3]

---

[2] In this, as in so much of the background to North Sea policy, the main light is cast in the evidence of officials to the Committee of Public Accounts, 1972/3.

[3] (*See facing page.*)

Although only an under-secretary in the Ministry of Power at the time, his knowledge of both exploration and the oil industry, gained through his training as a geographer and his experience as oil attaché in Washington and as chairman of the petroleum committee of the OEEC (the precursor to OECD), gave him an unusual degree of influence over policy formation and an unusually direct access ot Ministers. More than anything, an enthusiast for North Sea prospects and intensely patriotic, he was determined to get things moving and was equally determined, on the basis of his American experience, to ensure that development was as far as possible carried out by British companies and companies with sufficient technical and financial strength.

Mr. Beckett's views were supported by that discreet coincidence of Treasury and departmental thinking and the interests of large companies, which has so often been behind industrial policies in Britain. The advice of the inter-departmental committee established between the Ministry of Power, Treasury and Cabinet Office before the first round and thereafter was clear enough. The overriding need was for a balance of payments. This, in turn, implied as rapid a rate of exploration and development as possible and, as far as possible, a substantial British content to exploration.[4]

At the same time the Government was being advised by two committees drawn from oil industry representatives, on both the legal and licensing aspects of the first round. That these committees should be dominated by the major oil companies and that their voices should carry most weight with the Government, was hardly

---

[3] Mr. Beckett, who retired in 1972, has since been criticised strongly for giving away so much so cheaply to the oil companies. In some ways the criticism is inevitable, considering the degree of influence he had over policy and his own forceful beliefs, both in favour of rapid exploration (leading to the large size of the 1971/2 fourth round) and against state involvement (which brought him into conflict with Labour Ministers during the 1964-70 Government). But, in view of the general political apathy about the North Sea until late in the day and the lack of experience in the Ministry, it is doubtful whether the whole exercise would have got under way so rapidly without him. And to him, too, must go much of the credit for inducing so much exploration interest at times when the geological prospects and general oil price environment were not encouraging.

[4] As with so much in British economic policy, the basic assumptions about the primacy of balance of payments considerations never appear to have been fully tested at the time. Nor were the precise implications of off-shore exploration on the balance of payments ever worked out. Because of the immediate benefits to the capital account, the Treasury appears to have positively favoured foreign investment in the early years. The question of British content seems to have been largely a political and Ministry of Power concern.

surprising. The relationship between the oil companies and the civil service had traditionally been one where the Ministry of Power looked to the refiners (mainly the major companies) for investment and security of supply and the Treasury looked to Shell and BP for help in keeping their funds in sterling and co-operating on currency flows. The major companies, when asked for their advice on license allocation, argued strongly against the obvious alternative of an auction system in favour of a discretionary system on the not altogether disinterested grounds that a bidding system would reduce the funds available to companies for exploration work and would encourage the entry of companies without the resources or experience to develop finds they made or to stick with exploration if they had disappointing wells.

The result was a traditional English compromise. The North Sea was divided into a grid of 100 square mile blocks[5] which were put on offer to any U.K. registered company that could prove a reasonable degree of financial and technical competence (this was inserted to discourage pure investment consortia). Preference in the actual allocation—which was at the discretion of the Minister—would be given, however, on the grounds of "the contribution the applicant has already made and is making, towards the development of resources of our continental shelf and the development of our fuel economy" (another way of saying British companies and those with refineries would be favoured), as well as on the work programme of wells and seismic surveys that applicants were prepared to carry out.

The aim was quite clearly to favour British companies, not only by giving them the largest percentage possible of blocks (the British interest in the first round was 22·7 per cent), but also the best quality blocks; to weed out companies without the capability of exploration (though, in practice, Angus Beckett deliberately encouraged competition from smaller newcomers by giving them reasonable second-rank blocks); to create some sort of bidding through the offer of work programmes; and to preserve a system of reward and favours for future rounds. In so far as the question of tax was deliberated, it was considered that the combination of corporation tax at around

[5] The size of block was itself a compromise between suggestions by the oil companies ranging from half this size to ten times its size. The decision was finally made on the grounds of administrative convenience. It had originally been expected that the major companies, which had urged larger blocks and criticised the size later, would apply for groups. In the event they surprised the Ministry by scattering their applications.

50 per cent and royalties at the world average of 12·5 per cent would give a broad share of profits similar enough to those obtaining particularly in the Middle East, because gas itself would have to be sold to the state gas industry. Meanwhile rents were put at a fairly low level and companies had to return at least half their licenced territory after six years.[6]

The way towards licence allocation was opened up in 1964 by the Continental Shelf Act, which extended British sovereignty over the Continental Shelf area. The bill only just scraped into a busy parliamentary session, thanks to the dropping out of another Government bill and actual licence allocation was deliberately hurried through to ensure as the Conservative Minister of Power, F. J. Erroll, admitted afterwards that it was a *fait accompli* before elections were held. Virtually all the North Sea area available to the Government, before boundary agreements had been reached with its neighbours, was put on offer and 53 licences were granted, covering about 32,000 square miles, largely in the southern sector of the North Sea.

The discretionary system chosen was clearly vulnerable both to the charge of favouritism to the oil companies, since the allocation decision was made in private by the Government, and to the charge that it did not tackle seriously enough the question of taxation and "economic rent". But it was successful in attracting a surprisingly wide range of applicants. It has been used as the basis not only for all the British licence rounds since then, save for the brief experimental excursion into auctioning during the fourth round, but has also served as the original model for the Norwegian rounds (where allocations were first made in 1965), for the Dutch (originally proposed in 1964 but not offered until 1967 after a provision allowing for state participation in finds had been added) and later, for awards in Germany.

In Britain, as in the Netherlands, the election of a new Government committed to a greater degree of public ownership, changed the

[6] The companies can themselves choose which half to return. The idea was to ensure that they would explore their allocations within six years rather than to force a return of good acreage. "Chequerboarding", as practised in Canada (under which the licensee has to return part of his acreage on a commercial discovery or after a set period, leaving corridors between the retained blocks) was considered before the second round was issued. It was rejected on the grounds that it raised too many difficulties in practice and was unsuitable to off-shore operations (see memorandum by the Department of Trade and Industry to the Public Accounts Committee, December 13, 1972).

political environment soon after the first round was offered. Nevertheless, settlement of the boundary line with Norway and Denmark and Holland encouraged an early issue of further licences to fill the border lines and the Government offered a second round of licences, changed only as much as greater preference was given to the state industries as a criterion for allocation—a point which was supported in its turn by the National Coal Board's successful agreement to share in the Gulf and Allied Chemicals group.

It was after the discovery of gas at the end of 1965 and 1966 that the Government undertook a radical review of licensing options, working through a committee of departmental officials, chaired by the Department of Economic Affairs, and including the Cabinet Office and Treasury as well as the industrial ministries. Its work was undoubtedly pressured; by the sense of a gas boom that accompanied the series of major gas discoveries of the time; by the determination of some of the Party's advisers (particularly Lord Balogh) to increase the economic rent from the exercise and by the Labour Party's proposals, when in opposition, for a state National Hydrocarbons Council (an idea partly developed by Professor Peter Odell).

Yet, though various radical ideas were mooted, including that of buying out all existing licences and another idea for offering all new concessions to a grand British consortium of BP, Gas Council, NCB and possible Shell (an idea Shell and BP opposed), none came to anything. Lord Balogh, the key adviser, was more interested in ensuring a low price for gas than in promoting a state oil company—indeed, to some extent, he believed in, and admired, the international oil companies for their technical competence. To develop the North Sea itself the country would have had to divert substantial resources from other sectors of the economy and would have suffered considerable delays in doing so.

The civil service was against compulsory state participation in future rounds, partly out of prejudice, but partly out of a genuine belief that it would slow down development, would prove too costly and was irrelevant to the country's needs.[7] Parliament as a whole

---

[7] The innate conservatism of the officials concerned is partly a matter of generations. Since then, officials—especially in an essentially policy-making rather than executive department such as Energy—have become considerably more interventionist in approach. The dislike of state bodies such as the British National Oil Corporation remains, as much because they are difficult for Whitehall to control as that they are inefficient. For the history of the nationalised industry involvement in the North Sea, see the report of the Select Committee on Nationalised Industries (session 1974/5).

and the public were never very interested in licensing policy at all (the debates at the time were generally far more concerned with safety, law and prices than with overall policy). Successive Ministers of Power (Fred Lee, Richard Marsh and Harold Lever) were hardly enthusiastic for state participation. By the time the Government did get round to a third offer of licences in 1969, the exploration mood had in any event changed, as the phase of big discoveries gave way to smaller prospects for which the Gas Council's low price offered little inducement.

Thus, the third round of licences was built very much on the same terms and the same discretionary allocation system as the previous two. The round, for the first time, deliberately limited the number of blocks on offer. It opened up new areas to the west of the U.K. and, for the first time, required state participation in them. But in the North Sea proper, it contented itself with suggesting that preference would be given to those in partnership with the state. Otherwise, the royalty rates, the system of allocation and surrender terms (all issues which the inter-departmental committee had considered changing) were kept the same and only the rentals were slightly increased.

What had happened in between the second and third rounds of licences was a classic exploration cycle first of disappointment, then of major finds, then of a tailing-off in size of finds and of company enthusiasm, only on this occasion much accelerated. Less than a year and only half-a-dozen wells after the first hole was drilled in the U.K. North Sea in December 1964, BP had discovered an important gas field in its first well on block 48/6, the West Sole Field.

By the end of 1965, the Shell-Esso partnership had discovered an even larger field at Leman Bank (later confirmed as one of the largest off-shore gas fields anywhere in the world) and the Phillips group had found a small field named Ann on block 49/26. Over the following two years, the Indefatigable Field was found, as well as the Hewett Field (the latter came somewhat as a surprise on a block and in geological formations considered of little interest when the licences were allocated), and development plans were instituted for both the West Sole and Leman Bank Fields. To these were added, in 1968, the Viking and the Deborah Fields.

By the time the Ministry of Power had organised a grand meeting of representatives of all the energy industries, to hammer out its white paper on fuel policy—the meeting took place at Selsdon Park over a long weekend in May 1967 and the White Paper was published in

Autumn—it was possible to suggest that the southern sector of the U.K. North Sea might provide gas reserves of more than 20 trillion cubic feet and that, together with additional discoveries, this might support a plateau production of around 4,000m. cubic feet per day by the middle of the next decade—enough to triple the size of the industry's sales and give it more than 10 per cent of the country's total primary energy market at a saving of several hundred million pounds on the balance of payments each year.

The central questions raised were the price which the Gas Corporation, as an effective monopoly purchaser of the gas, would have to pay and the rate at which the gas ought to be developed. Although the two questions were clearly connected—the lower the price the faster it could be pushed into the market—it was the price question which dominated the headlines at the time.

Four months after the discovery of the West Sole Field, BP reached provisional agreement with the Gas Council in February 1966, for a delivered price for West Sole gas of 5 old pence (2·08p) per thousand cubic feet (a therm) for the first three years of a 15-year contract. The price appears to have been very much a back-of-the-envelope compromise between the production cost of gas and the price it might fetch on the open market compared to oil (then considered to be around 6 to 7 old pence per therm).

At the time, Ministers made it clear that this price was not to be taken as the measure for future agreements, but it was sufficiently high to encourage companies to go ahead with development plans for other fields such as Leman Bank. Great was their shock, therefore when they met the Gas Council in Spring, to be told that the Gas Council's offer was 1·8 old pence per therm (0·75p). Thus the scene was set for two years of bitter negotiations, during which the oil companies proceeded with development plans, finding them more and more difficult to cancel as the negotiations got tougher, while the price issue itself developed into a major political issue on which the Government felt it difficult to compromise.

Essentially, the argument was between the Gas Council's view, backed strongly by Lord Balogh, that the price ought to be settled on a "cost plus" basis and the oil companies' view, that it should be related to the price of competitive energy forms. The argument was made more intense by the fact that, because of the nature of off-shore exploration and development, the oil companies were looking for prices which would enable them to install capacity on the basis of the full life and flows of a field. However, any price also directly influenced the incentives which companies without finds would need to encourage them to explore for new and perhaps smaller fields.

The Gas Council did, early on, offer a deal, under which it would pay for tranches of gas as and when it needed them, but this was quickly rejected by the oil companies as being unworkable, in view of their need to develop a field as a whole. The argument therefore proceeded, with the Gas Council not only seeking a cost plus formula (which it could calculate through its own share in the Amoco group which held part of the Leman and Indefatigable Fields), but also requiring a low price if it was to proceed with a massive conversion exercise and buy its way into a market which was then suffering from low prices brought about by new oil supplies from Libya. The oil companies, for their part, sought some relation between the gas sales price and comparable market prices. But their bargaining position was weakened, both by their existing commitment to development programmes and by their interest in seeing as rapid a rate of production as possible, to justify their investment.

In the end, there was a rough and not wholly satisfactory compromise as the two sides moved their figures either way. A study, commissioned by the inter-departmental committee looking into North Sea questions, showed that, on a price of 3 old pence and high reserves, a discounted cash flow return of 18·5 per cent might result, although the figures would be lower for new reserves. The Gas Corporation, left to itself, seemed ready to move towards that sort of figure and, during 1967, the two sides appear to have been ready to sign an agreement at around 3·2 old pence per therm. However, the decision was referred to Cabinet (the political interest in the negotiations had been close from the start), who promptly refused the agreement, putting the whole negotiation back into the melting pot. After a further period of hard bargaining, the Government was able to divide the oil companies with the threat that it would not buy gas from some of the smaller fields if agreement was not reached. Fearful of this, Arpet and Phillips, with the threatened Hewett Field, gave in and signed early in 1968 at a price of 2·87d. (1·25p) per therm.

The other companies soon followed and (although slightly higher prices were settled for the Indefatigable Field, which was further from shore and for the Viking Field, which was not developed until the turn of the decade) this price became the basis for most of the industry's supplies.

The low price, as it turned out, did affect exploration and later left the Gas Council in an awkward supply hiatus during 1974-5.

But it did enable the gas industry to go for an extremely ambitious programme of conversion to natural gas and market expansion. Its decision to do this proved one of the most important, and most effectively carried out industrial acts since the War. At the time it was hardly debated in public at all, although bitterly opposed by Lord Robens,[8] then chairman of the Coal Board.

It was a decision which clearly had the support of the Treasury, which wanted the maximum balance of payments impact, and of the oil companies, who wanted rapid development of fields, in view of the high initial capital costs of production. But this should not detract from the courage of the gas industry's approach. Having suffered for a decade as the poor relation of the fuel industries and having, at one time, faced the feeling in the Treasury, at least, that it should be contracted, it had already taken considerable steps to preserve its position *vis-à-vis* North Sea gas, by means of imports (it was the first customer of liquid natural gas in the world) and conversion of its manufacturing processes from coal to oil. Once natural gas had been discovered and the quantities had proved large, the gas industry decided to move to total conversion within the relatively short space of ten years.

This approach was considerably more ambitious than had been practised elsewhere, such as in Germany, France or Australia, where natural gas had been introduced in phases, first being delivered directly to a power station and a few large industrial users in an area and then gradually being provided to domestic customers. Critics, particularly from the coal lobby, have argued that a much slower pace would have been more appropriate in the case of the U.K. They argue that gas should have been phased in over a longer period and that the industry should have continued to manufacture gas from coal.

But there were only two viable alternatives to conversion. The first was to continue transforming natural gas into gas of "town gas" quality, which would have entailed sizeable additional investment in plant, as well as wasting the opportunities of doubling the effective capacity of existing distribution lines by using natural gas direct (since each cubic foot of natural gas gives around twice the

---

[8] See Lord Robens' autobiography *Ten Year Stint* (1972) and the evidence of both the Coal Board and the Gas Council to the Select Committee on Nationalised Industries, which the exploitation of North Sea Gas (session 1967-8). For the economic considerations surrounding the Gas Council's investment decisions on conversion and transmission, see G. L. Reid's chapter on the gas industry in *The National Fuel Industries* (1973).

1967 White Paper Estimates of Gas Sales

(*million therms*)

Outcome in brackets for 1970/1 and 1975/6 financial years

	1966 (*actual*)	1970	1975
Domestic	2,147	3,600 (3,653)	5,100 (5,941)
Industrial	935	1,900 (1,704)	3,800 (5,172)
Commercial *et al.*	547	750 (775)	1,000 (1,400)
Power Stations	—	—	3,400 (900)
Total	3,656	8,300 (6,133)	13,300 (13,453)

heat of manufactured gas). The second alternative was to feed it into large plants in the initial stages, which would have meant its being given its lowest value-added use. At any reasonable calculation of marginal long-run costs, natural gas conversion was bound to be a better proposition than continuing with manufactured gas or developing imported gas, quite apart from the balance of payments benefits. As long as this was so, rapid development at a low initial raw material cost made sense as the best way of justifying the massive initial investment costs of creating a transmission system for natural gas (initially estimated at around £1,200m. over a five-year period) and conversion (at an initial estimated cost of £400m. over a ten-year period).

In the event, the gas industry did over extend itself. Conversion proved a more difficult operation than first expected. Costs were higher. The target of tripling sales within seven to eight years caused the industry to sell at low prices into the bulk markets. This, coupled with higher than expected investment costs, in turn, greatly reduced the industry's ability to deliver the substantial reduction in prices over the longer term which it had initially promised its customers. It also had the effect of priming demand to a point which it was then unable to supply in the mid-seventies.

In the same way, the rapid development of off-shore fields, in sea, weather and seabed conditions more relentless than the oil industry had previously experienced, brought major problems in the loss of rigs, in the supply of pipe and in platform corrosion. The pace of ordering caught much of British industry off balance and unwilling or unable to meet demand to supply.

In some ways, it could be argued that to have fixed a higher price of gas at the time would have eased the supply hiatus problems in the mid-seventies and might have resulted in a slightly slower pace of market penetration. But events since then have tended to justify the initial decision to embark on total conversion. The rapid development of gas in the late sixties has brought to the customers and to the economy, benefits of very considerable importance during the troubled times of the 1970s. Drilling since then has suggested that there will be sufficient reserves to see the industry through to the 1990s without great difficulty. After the cost and oil price explosions of 1974/75, it is hard to avoid drawing the conclusion that the gas development is one of the very few examples in Britain of a new resource resulting in productive investment within the country—a situation which would not have necessarily occured if the economic rent had been taken in taxation.

These points about the gas phase of North Sea development are worth making. During that time, Britain enjoyed a period of offshore development which no other European country had; experienced (indeed, in all the other sectors, only the small trouble-ridden Dan oil field off Denmark was brought into development).

Against the general background of falling energy prices, intense oil competition, and the impact of new low-cost resources from North Africa and the Middle East, British licensing policy did encourage a surprisingly high rate of exploration and production certainly it encouraged a more rapid move from initial discovery to production than had been experienced in other oil provinces), while the nationalised gas industry's marketing and distribution policy ensured a rapid impact on-shore.

But the experience also forewarned of the pattern that was to occur with oil. On the exploration side, initial failures were followed speedily by a period of major finds giving rise to a sense of euphoria that was then deflated by a period of decline in reserve additions and growing worries about the pace of drilling. On the development side, the problems of translating into the extreme conditions of the North Sea technology built up in other areas became all too clear, even in the relatively shallow depths of the southern sector of the North Sea. The poverty of British industry's response to the new market for goods and services was soon apparent, despite initial successes in building rigs. Apparent too, in retrospect, has been the relatively small impact on general economic trends of the North Sea gas development, despite its relative importance in the energy field.

If some of the same mistakes and misapprehensions have occurred since, in the oil phase, nobody can say that the country should not have been warned by its first experiences.

2 Oil Takes Over

The discovery of oil in the North Sea radically altered the pattern of the North Sea development game and the enthusiasm of its players. For the exploration industry, oil presented quite a different target from gas. In comparison with gas, which, because of its nature, has to be piped to shore and, in the European circumstances, sold to a monopoly distributor, oil is eminently flexible. It can be transported by tanker or pipeline and shipped anywhere in the world. It commands a price laid down by world market conditions and, of not least importance to the major oil companies dominating North Sea production, it provides a secure source for their own "downstream" operations in refining and marketing. Even if the cost of off-shore exploration had made North Sea oil uncompetitive as against alternative Middle East sources, the major companies would still have been interested lest its discovery promoted protectionist policies by consumer governments which could leave their own supply position vulnerable.

Why the oil industry had not expected the series of major finds eventually discovered remains an open question. Nobody likes to admit their mistakes, particularly oil companies. Yet there were few who believed that the North Sea would become an important oil province. Surprisingly some of the major companies such as BP, Mobil and Texaco showed signs of distinct disenchantment with U.K. North Sea exploration at the time the first oil finds were made.[1] There were still fewer who expected it to become one of the most important new oil provinces to be discovered since the Second World War.

Part of the reason was a matter for the commercial interests and attitudes of the companies concerned. An oil company works on annual budgeting for its different functions and the degree to which it puts resources into exploitation in any one area reflects both its

---

[1] Clive Callow in *Power from the Sea* (Gollancz, 1973) quotes Sir Eric Drake, chairman of BP, as predicting in April 1970, that there would not be a major oil field in the North Sea, only six months before his company found the Forties Field.

view of geology and, just as important, its particular requirements for oil. The late sixties had seen oil company returns in the market place and prices suffer from a growing glut of oil from the Middle East and Africa. Companies like Gulf, BP and Texaco had more than enough oil for their own requirements and therefore had less enthusiasm to spend a lot of money on new finds. Even other companies like Shell and to some extent Esso, who were "crude short", had limited enthusiasm for an expensive investment at a time when the costs of producing oil from deep water and far from the shore seemed barely likely to compete with traditional sources.

But part of the reason also was a question of geological knowledge. It would be untrue to say that the oil industry didn't expect to find oil in the North Sea. Oil is found across a wide variety of regions of the world. It existed on-shore Germany and Britain. Some of the early wells such as the first wells in 1966 and 1967 in the Danish sector, Esso's 25/11 in the Norwegian sector drilled in 1967 and Burmah's well in U.K. waters on block 48/17 in the same year all tested oil in small quantities.

It was more a matter of whether commercial oil fields, in the sense of large enough reservoirs to justify production, would be discovered than whether oil would be found at all. The problem was that the northern parts of the North Sea were largely unknown. The theory of Continental Drift (the slow splitting of continents from each other millions of years ago), still less the concept of plate tectonics or sea-floor spreading, was only just beginning to take hold of the attitudes of the oil companies.

Certainly there were enthusiasts among exploration geologists. Both Shell and Total, for example, appear to have taken licences in the far north off the Shetlands and the Orkneys earlier than anyone else in the second and third rounds, at least partly because of a feeling that the geology might be closely connected with the more attractive geology of on-shore Greenland. But for the industry as a whole the knowledge of on-shore conditions on either side of the North Sea was not sufficiently helpful or encouraging to suggest that large oil deposits might lie off-shore. Early seismic surveys suggested substantial thicknesses of Tertiary deposits, where most of the world's oil is found. But some felt that the conditions thought to be necessary for oil generation were not present at that period in north-west Europe, while nothing discovered during drilling through the younger rocks in search of gas in the southern sector suggested the conditions of reservoir rock or depth of burial were right for large finds in the North Sea—indeed, the opposite was felt to be true. On the evidence of the on-shore Midlands fields and the early wells off Norway and Denmark, all the signs were that any oil found would be in small accumulations unconducive to commercial off-shore fields.

As with the Groningen discovery in the history of gas exploration, so was oil exploration immeasurably accelerated by a major oil discovery. This time it was by the Phillips group at Ekofisk off Norway. Rumours about potential oil finds had been circulating ever since the group had tested gas and condensate from Lower Tertiary sandstones in the Cod Field in 1968. But further drilling in the area proved both difficult and interesting rather than rewarding until, in April 1970, the group, close to giving up on its long search, completed and tested a highly promising second well on the Ekofisk structure in the southern part of the Norwegian sector.

The results immediately indicated a potentially large field in the world "giant" class (fields with 1,000m. barrels of recoverable oil or more which account for around two-thirds of the world's oil reserves). Although the reservoir conditions suggested problems and the group was initially cautious, reports of the find in the industry and remarks made by some of the partners galvanised the industry in the North Sea and among North American companies who had yet to take an interest in the area.

Even so, the unique and geographically limited presence of the Danian and Upper Cretaceous limestone reservoir rocks in which the gas was found did not immediately imply similar finds would be made in the U.K. sector. Although the Amoco-Gas Council group found an interesting Tertiary sandstone field at Montrose off the Scottish coast in 1969, it was not until BP discovered in October 1970 a major field of world class at Forties north-east of Aberdeen that the real proof of British potential came. The Forties discovery, finally declared a commercial discovery in the next year, was followed in the next nine months by further discoveries by Shell-Esso at Auk, the Phillips group at Josephine in the U.K. sector and, of greatest importance of all although kept highly secret at the time, by Shell-Esso at Brent in June 1971 in an entirely different basin east of the Shetlands.

By this time, with a new Conservative Government in office and the Ministry of Power merged into a new department under an ex-oil executive, Mr. John Davies, the Government had decided on issuing a further major round—the much criticised and most dramatic fourth round. For the first time it conducted, as part of this round, an experimental auction of 15 blocks of varying location and quality. For the first time it opened entirely new areas west of the Shetlands and south-west of Wales. But otherwise, the licence terms, the discretionary allocation system and the surrender clauses remained virtually the same as previously.

Under stinging criticism from the House of Commons' Public Accounts Committee a year later, the Department of Trade and Industry (which had taken over the Ministry of Power) argued that a fall in the number of rigs operating in U.K. waters during 1970/1 had been behind its decision to gear-up exploration in quite such a dramatic fashion. This may have some truth to it as there were fears that the finds in both the Norwegian and, to some extent the Dutch sectors, were drawing away interest in the U.K. sector; there were worries that recent actions by the Organisation of Petroleum Exporting Countries to raise prices would induce a flow of rigs to the U.S. and to potential oil areas off Asia; and there had been a decline in rig activity as companies came to the end of their drilling obligations in the southern sector of the North Sea.[2]

But the more likely reason is the opposite—that once oil had been found in the U.K. sector in northern waters, the Government became desperately anxious to find out as quickly as it could what was there. Its knowledge of prospects, indeed the general knowledge of the industry as a whole, was rudimentary. Detailed assessment of potential oil traps, even with extensive seismic information available (as there was), could only be built up as wells were drilled to correlate the seismic picture with positive drilling experience of the various rock strata and as the results of these wells were traded. In northern waters, the necessary pattern of wells simply had not been drilled by 1971.[3]

Shaken by events in the Middle East, where first Libya and then

---

[2] The number of exploration and appraisal wells drilled in a year had fallen from 47 in 1969/70 to 22 in 1970/1, while mobile rig activity, in rig years, fell from 7·7 in 1969 to 5·3 in 1970 and 5·2 in 1972.

[3] The technical competence of the Ministry to assess the information was undoubtedly weak. Although all companies had to provide the Government with their seismic and drilling results, these were handed on to the Institute of Geological Sciences—an academic institution with limited expertise in petroleum geology. The number of technical staff in the petroleum division of the relevant ministry was still only 6 in 1970 and 7 in 1971 and was half this in the preceding years. Further, the rules covering exploration allowed companies to keep well logs a commercial secret far longer than in other countries (although this has since been changed).

OPEC as a whole had been able to take advantage of marginal shortages of tankers and refining capacity to raise prices in the Teheran and Tripoli negotiations of 1971; pulled along by the new Government's policy of breaking out into rapid economic growth; politically anxious to give as many areas of Britain as possible, including Wales, a chance to join in and also fearful that only a dramatic move could arouse the interest of British industry, the Government went for a major round covering as many areas as possible.

The interest of the Department of Trade and Industry was to see what Britain had got, as rapidly as possible. The Treasury interest, as ever, was to make as strong and as early an impact on the balance of payments as possible. The political interest was to help create an atmosphere of growth and expansion. With limited geological knowledge, the auction was regarded not as a way of determining economic rent for future rounds but as a consciously experimental way of testing relative interest and hence was included as part of the main discretionary round not as a precursor. The question of taxation, it was felt once more, could be left until actual discoveries were made. The political sensitivities were hardly present since, save for a few exceptions such as Lord Balogh, the size and terms of the round aroused little parliamentary interest or criticism at the time.

If the object of the exercise was to promote rapid exploration, it succeeded beyond anyone's expectations. Allocation of the bulk of the discretionary licences (the auction had been held in August 1971) was made in 1972. By that time exploration activity was picking up rapidly, checked only through the availability of large semi-submersible rigs capable of drilling in deep water. During 1971, in addition to the Shell-Esso Auk and Brent finds (confirmed at first by implication when Shell-Esso bid an astonishing £21m. for a neighbouring block during the auction), the Hamilton Brothers group confirmed a find at Argyll, Amoco confirmed its find at Montrose and BP confirmed the size of its Forties Field.

Already it was clear that the U.K. was within reach of enough oil to make it self-sufficient through the 1980s. The next year 1972-1973, proved even better—the "anni mirabiles" of oil exploration—as the rigs concentrated their attention on northern waters, particularly east of the Shetlands, and as the rate of discovery increased to around one success in four wells drilled.

Shell-Esso, although unsuccessful in their drilling on the "golden" auction block for which it had paid so much, nonetheless added another potentially important oil field to its catch at Cormorant, while Mobil discovered the Beryl Field, Occidental the Piper Field and Total the Frigg gas field all during 1972. In 1973, further fields in the East Shetlands area were added by Shell-Esso again at Dunlin, by Burmah-Signal at Thistle, by Unocal at Heather, by Conoco/NCB at Hutton and by Total at Alwyn while off the mainland of Scotland, the Phillips group established the Maureen Field. Production plans were announced for Forties, Brent, Auk, Beryl and Piper. The pace continued through 1974 with finds becoming rather smaller and development programmes pushing ahead. While the companies themselves remained initially cautious about stating the size of individual fields, few disputed that the northern section of the North Sea had now become a major oil province of world standards, capable of producing enough if not more than enough to meet U.K. requirements, and of immense potential significance to its balance of payments.

Yet the speed of this development also brought its own problems. One was simply that of digestion for the oil companies themselves and the industries which served them. The intensity of exploration and the unprecedented eagerness which the companies showed in arranging development plans after only a few exploration wells had been drilled on a structure masked the degree of challenge in producing from such deep and hostile waters. Production from around 300 feet had been successfully established elsewhere. But the finds, particularly off the Shetlands, were in water depths of well over 400 feet in most cases, they were at least 100 miles from the shore and they were in sea and weather conditions remarkable as much for the continuous pressure on structures as for the appalling winter conditions when off-shore work was often impossible for long months.

In a sense the industry, and the country, was a victim of its own success. The pace of exploration led from the start to a rapid escalation in rental costs for rigs and a surge of rig orders for yards in the U.S., Canada, Norway and Japan (whilst British yards proved largely uninterested). The production programmes got into far greater difficulties. The pipe-laying barges, the derrick barges for installation and the construction capacity for building major platform structures were all in short supply. Much of the existing off-shore equipment could not work through winter conditions, particularly in the north. The oil companies changed their designs as they went along. British construction facilities, inheriting many of the traditional problems of shipyards, were soon cast down by inter-union disputes. Costs rocketed by as much as 200 per cent in some cases. The development programme for virtually every field was delayed by a year and in some cases by as much as two years. North Sea oil, which had been expected to make its initial impact in 1974, slipped back to 1975 and then to 1976. The Government, seriously concerned about the number of orders going abroad, set up new supervisory mechanisms in the Off-Shore Supplies Office and started to finance with public money new facilities in Scotland. The oil companies, shaken by their experience, began to re-assess the pace of development and the expected cash flows and returns.[4]

More important, the speed and success of exploration also aroused—as it has done in every oil area of the world—a political backlash of concern about profits and depletion. The problem of taxing North Sea oil profits and the criticism beginning to emerge over the "give-away" nature of the fourth round had already caused the Government to set up an inter-departmental committee between the Industry Department and the Treasury in 1972 by the time that the Public Accounts Committee ("PAC"), prodded by Lord Balogh and other critics, commenced its investigations that year.

By the time the PAC really got into the crucial question of tax during its examination in the winter of 1972/3, the Government had already produced preliminary plans for tightening tax controls and ensuring that companies would not be able to set North Sea profits against other worldwide losses. The Government thinking appears to have been to let the PAC produce its criticisms and then neatly to jump straight in with the answer already planned for the 1973 budget. If so, the Government fell flat on its face. The PAC, with evidence that the two British companies, Shell and BP, alone had amassed £1,500m. in artificial tax losses on their Middle East operation which could theoretically be set against North Sea profits,[5] made the issue into a grand scandal, criticising not only the tax offset position but also implying that the Government had failed to extract nearly enough in royalties, rents or surrender provisions. The feeling that the Government had indulged in a monstrous

[4] Not the least serious part of this surge in activity was the rise in number of accidents as the production programme got under way. Fatalities, which were at a level of 3 a-year in 1972 and 1973, shot up to 12 in 1974, 10 in 1975 and 20 in 1976, including 7 divers and 10 workers on rigs and platforms. Serious accidents over the same period rose from 17 in 1972 to 22 in 1973, 25 in 1974, 50 in 1975 and 57 in 1976.

[5] (*See facing page.*)

give-away in the fourth round was only strengthened by events across the North Sea, where the Norwegian Government was moving to impose compulsory state participation in new licences, to slow down development and to set up a state corporation of its own.[6]

The PAC's suggestion of a barrelage tax (an additional straight duty payment on each barrel produced according to production levels) was bitterly disputed by the oil companies over the summer, when the question was given an entirely new dimension by the oil crisis of October 1973 and the quadrupling of prices by OPEC in that winter. The Inland Revenue was set the task of producing ideas for an excess profits tax to cream off these "windfall profits" when the political parameters were again changed by the election of a new Labour Government in February 1974, committed not only to higher taxation but also to taking the whole North Sea development into public ownership.

---

[5] *First Report from the Committee of Public Accounts,* session 1972/3. The theoretical losses arose from the particular nature of the posted price system in the Middle East. Middle East taxes were levied on a notional price (the posted price) which was then the price at which the oil was sold to the trading company of the international oil group. Since this price was higher than the market price, however, at some point in the group's system the price had to be marked down to a realistic level, thus incurring a book loss for the company by the time the oil was sold to the final consumer. These losses could, under U.K. law, be set against any profits made by the company in Britain. The losses, confined to U.K. based oil groups (U.S. companies naturally preferred to offset against U.S. tax), were of relatively small importance to the U.K. Treasury before the North Sea development since generous British investment allowances ensured that few oil companies made much taxable profit out of U.K. refining and marketing operations. Once North Sea exploration developed, however, they were clearly of much more importance. How far British companies really expected to use them is obscure. Shell's chairman at the time said not; BP indicated that it did expect to. By the time the PAC started its hearings, however, an inter-departmental committee was already established to tighten the rules.

[6] The Norwegian Government had moved to introduce a right to a state share in net profits or an equity share in any finds, as well as renewing certain "key" blocks for the stake, as part of the licence round of 1969 (although most of the share rights negotiated with the companies were relatively small). With the establishment of a major group of finds in the Ekofisk area, there was a rising political call for more control. State participation was introduced when licence changes were sought, or when, as in the case of Phillips' plans to pipe Ekofisk oil to Teesside were discussed, an export licence was needed. By 1972/3, when the Phillips proposals were discussed and a new licence round debated, the Norwegian Government had moved far towards introducing royalty rates and tougher terms (in the Royal Decree of 8th December 1972) and towards a policy of "make haste slowly" (reducing the pace of new licence allocations, putting a limit on production and reserving acreage for the state) as set out in the crucial reports to Parliament by the Finance Ministry (Report 25 in session 1973/4) and the Industry Department (Report 30, 1973/4).

Thence ensued an extraordinary—and in many ways comic—period of political confusion and negotiating tension with the oil companies as the Labour Government attempted to put into practice its vague concepts of increasing the public control and share in the new resources against a background of parliamentary weakness, rising Scottish nationalism, a changing world environment on energy, increasing worries over costs and delays on production programmes and a tapering-off in the rate of additional reserves brought about by new exploration.

The Government's first, and inevitable move, was to separate the question of tax from those of state participation and control. In theory there was a good case for keeping them all together. A greater share in profits can as easily be achieved through a state share in equity as higher taxes. Given that any share in equity and change in rules of control had to be negotiated retrospectively, there could have been a good negotiating case for playing one off against another.[7]

It was never really considered. The traditional Treasury desire to keep tax questions unto themselves was backed by a distinctly luke-warm attitude by many Cabinet members to the question of state participation anyway and this in turn was buttressed by the political weakness of the Government's position in Parliament. From the beginning, therefore, Mr. Edmund Dell, who was handling the tax question as Paymaster General in the Treasury, went for an early resolution of the tax problem in isolation from other questions.

Over the summer of 1974, the Inland Revenue developed its own ideas of a tax that could be levied on companies to increase the Government's share of profits and ensure that there were no loop-holes through which the oil companies could slip and, by the time

---

[7] The broad outlines of the new Government's policy towards the North Sea were published in a brief and very generalised report to Parliament in July 1974, setting out its wish for higher taxes, a state corporation, greater control and "voluntary" participation in past licences. Closure of the tax loopholes was first set in motion by the Chancellor's budget that year and was followed by the Petroleum Revenue Tax proposals, informally circulated to oil companies in the Autumn, and presented to Parliament in November 1974. The rate of tax proposed was not announced until early the following year and the bill was finally passed in Spring 1975. Participation talks meanwhile began in November of 1974. A few months earlier companies were circulated with the Government's broad proposals for greater control over operations, developed in the Petroleum and Submarine Pipe-Lines Bill published in April of 1975 and passed in November that year. The outlines, and safeguards, of the Government's policy on refining and depletion controls were meanwhile announced in December 1974.

the election was held in October which gave the Government a more comfortable majority, the Inland Revenue was ready with a preliminary draft which it handed out for the oil companies' and bankers' comments.

The Inland Revenue was motivated partly by its lack of knowledge and long-felt resentment of the international oil companies, partly by its wish for a tax that would be relatively simple to administer and partly by its traditional passion for preventing tax avoidance rather than creating taxes which would induce activity.[8] Just as in the days of the gas tax, the government attitude was one of ensuring the maximum "take" from existing fields, whether or not this would have a negative effect on fields still to be found and developed.

The proposals, officially kept secret, brought immediate cries of horror from the exploration industry, although some of the major companies appear to have been consulted before the letter was sent out. Companies without finds, or with small finds of marginal commercial prospects, were quick to point out that the single rate approach failed to reflect their particular problems or the dramatic rate of inflation which made such a significant difference to costs according to the timing of each development. Large companies objected to the concept of separating fields for the purposes of the new tax rather than allowing companies to set off development in one field against cash flow from another. Smaller companies felt that they had been betrayed by the larger companies, which, with existing major fields, were less worried about the effect of a single rate of tax on smaller finds and new exploration.

Their discomfort was made all the greater when the proposals for the new tax, to be called the Petroleum Revenue Tax, were formally published in November 1974 and it was seen that little of substance had been changed from the draft proposals and virtually

[8] The Inland Revenue, although part of the Treasury in terms of ministerial responsibility, has always jealously guarded its independence. It has consistently followed the unreal argument that the question of the incentive/disincentive role of tax is for the Treasury while the question of imposition was that of the Inland Revenue. In the case of the Petroleum Revenue Tax proposals its inherent attitudes to tax were largely responsible for rejecting the concept of a profits tax in favour of a single rate tax (for administrative ease) while its lack of contact with developments in the North Sea and its tendency to confine its contacts in the industry to the major oil companies seems to have made it unaware of the problems of cost escalation, the differences in returns between fields, the problems of financing etc. which were to dominate the arguments once the bill was published.

none of the industry's objections had been taken into account. In the fierce lobbying that ensued not only from the oil companies but their bankers and British industrialists worried about the fall off in orders, virtually everyone was brought in. The Cabinet Policy Review Staff (the "Think Tank" set up by Edward Heath) made a quick study of its own and urged radical changes in the proposed tax.

Mr. Dell intervened and—in a move which to all appearances seems to have been almost unprecedented—the tax question and the negotiations with the companies seem to have been taken out of the hands of the Inland Revenue directly into the hands of the Treasury, aided by a specially formed committee on which two representatives of the oil industry (BP and Exxon) were seconded to hammer out changes with the Treasury under-secretary, Mr. Leon Pliatzky. As with a number of other bills before Parliament at the time, the committee stage proved to be not one of minor adjustments but major changes to the form of the bill. The "principles" of the new tax—a single rate levied on a field-by-field assessment of cash flow—remained the same. But the reality of the proposals were fundamentally altered in the direction of great flexibility by the introduction of larger offsets, a capital "uplift" to enable rapid repayment of initial investment, a production allowance and a safety net clause to relieve the incidence of the tax altogether if returns fell below a stated level.

In the meantime, the direct sponsoring department for oil (devolved once more into a separate Department of Energy during the oil crisis of 1973/74), was going through a similar exercise in negotiations, tension and compromise, clause by clause in its proposals for more direct control over depletion rates, investment, direction of oil flows and its use in refineries as covered by the Petroleum and Submarine Pipelines Bill (itself preceded by a consultative letter to the companies). The Department's aim was to recover itself from the lack of initial control contained in the licence rounds and to put itself in a position where all government ministries like to be—flexible controls to be turned on or off as development progresses. This inevitably cuts directly across the industry's desire for a degree of certainty and commercial discretion of their own in planning and carrying out long-term investments, with the result that prolonged periods of haggling went on to limit the Government's powers of intervention without appeal and to ensure that action could not be taken that would *post facto* undermine commercial returns.

Once the decisions to pursue increasing tax and control had been made separately, the questions of the appropriation of a state oil company and a state participation of 51 per cent in all existing fields (both announced as intended measures at the same time as the tax and control legislation) were ignored. The creation of a state oil company, the British National Oil Corporation (BNOC), was viewed with some suspicion by both the Department of Energy, because it might diminish its powers of control, and the Treasury, which was worried about cost. It raised fears in the industry that it could distort prices and returns by competing in the market place on a non-commercial basis, and it aroused the traditional parliamentary conflicts over state intervention.

The solution, as in the other cases, was found in a compromise form of unusual qualifications and an unusual lack of definition. A Corporation was established, but Parliament was assured that it would not act uncommercially. The question of refining and marketing was left open with a vague statement that it would not occur for some years anyway. The financial disciplines were imposed through the creation of a curious National Oil Account system, into which all state revenues from oil would be paid and out of which the Corporation would take what it required as it needed it (rather than the normal form of a Corporation with a set budget and targets). The civil servants' interests were maintained by a number of statements making the new corporation more regularly accountable both to the Minister and to Parliament and by the presence of two officials (from the Department of Energy and Treasury) on the board of the new Corporation. Whether the Corporation was to act as an independent company on the lines of British Freight for example, or as an arm of Government policy was simply left open.

The fruition of this line of approach, although hardly the answer to the oustanding questions by it, came with the announcement of a new round of licences offered in the summer of 1976 and finally allocated early in 1977 (the delay was partly attributable to the problems of gaining participation with some of the applicants). One reason for the round was simply to establish politically a change in ground rules and a tougher approach. Another was to present a carrot for participation in existing licences. A third was to offset the first gesture in a new policy of controlling, as the Norwegians had done, the pace of exploration and development by controlling the rate of new licence awards.

With these factors in mind, coupled with the simple fact that most of the best acreage had already been awarded in the previous round, the fifth round was a deliberately limited one, containing 71 blocks compared to the total 436 offered in the fourth round. New areas were opened up both in the Channel and in the Western Approaches area south and south-west of Cornwall. The financial terms on rentals and the licence surrender terms were stiffened (companies had to return two-thirds of their licences after seven years instead of a half after six years as previously).

But intriguingly, royalty rates were not changed (although the basis of their calculation was altered), nor was the basic method of discretionary allocation. Instead the major innovation was that applicants had to offer BNOC (or the Gas Corporation) at least a 51 per cent share of the licence although—a mark of the Government's determination to make the round a success in the face of uneven interest by the companies—the Government backed down from its initial demand that BNOC be "financially carried" through the development phase and instead suggested that it pay its way through all phases.[9]

Negotiations on majority state participation in all fields meanwhile took a great deal longer for the simple reason that, in the first place, the Government had little idea of what it wanted and, in the second, the separate imposition of new tax and control legislation left it with precious little negotiating power. For reasons of good faith, the continued need to encourage foreign investment and technology, the lack of British ability to pay its way and fear of almost certain ramifications from abroad at any retroactive compulsion (BP played strongly the card of possible action against its Alaska assets), the Government had to make negotiations voluntary. Without compulsion and with the tax side already arranged, it then proceeded with an offer guaranteeing the companies a "no-gain-

---

[9] The concept of "carried interest", developed particularly by the Norwegians in Europe but already common practice in the newer licence allocations in Iran and other Middle Eastern countries, allows the state to "buy in" to a certain percentage of any find once a commercial discovery has been made whilst being "carried" through the exploration stages, and thus the high risk part. Once the find has been made, under Norwegian and Dutch rules, the state pays its full share of costs, including exploration expenditure. The U.K. Government's initial proposal that BNOC should be "carried through" the development stage as well would have made it virtually an extra profits tax. Its final decision to forego being carried through exploration—which the industry may well have accepted—seems to have arisen as much from BNOC's own pride and determination to be seen standing on its own feet as from the Government's desire to mollify the oil companies.

no-loss" agreement under which they would lose none of the profit from 49 per cent private ownership than they had originally expected from 100 per cent.

The offer dumbfounded the industry as much as it puzzled the public and the City and it has taken virtually two years to translate it to even the beginnings of broad agreement with the major oil field producers. As at first elaborated by the negotiating team, consisting of Mr. Dell, Mr. Harold Lever and Lord Balogh reporting to Mr. Eric Varley as Energy Secretary at the time, the offer consisted of a complex scheme under which the Government would pay its share of production costs from whatever time it joined in a development and would then pay back to the companies their lost share of profits minus an interest charge of the state's contribution to investment. The oil, it was promised, would be sold back to the companies at least for a preliminary period. The only carrot attached was the offer of preferential treatment in the next round of licences, then planned for 1976. The only stick involved was the veiled threat that rejection of this reasonable approach would only increase political calls for more drastic action to take over the industry.

The offer, largely the idea of Mr. Lever, was met with a good deal of suspicion from the more important companies. Most of them were doubtful whether it would prove workable in practice. The American companies in particular felt that, as long as the offer was voluntary, there was nothing in it to entice them to join the game, particularly as the next round of licences did not seem likely to include all that much of attractive territory. A few companies felt that the offer could not provide them with the political security that might form the most positive reason for accepting, and they feared that it would only be upset with time, especially in view of the outright scorn it aroused amongst the Conservative opposition in Parliament.

After months of hard bargaining, visits to the U.S. by Ministers and discreet chats with oil company chairmen, the only results by the end of 1975 were the acceptance in principle of the offer by a few "distress item" companies who had no real alternative, such as Tricentrol, which needed Government guarantees to raise its part of the Thistle Field development costs, Burmah, which had been forced to agree the principle as part of its Bank of England rescue operation (it later sold its share in the Thistle Field and other acreage to BNOC in any case) and a few companies such as Deminex, which needed Government permission to buy out additional holdings in the North Sea from other companies.

At this point the negotiating team was changed by the addition of Lord Kearton, newly-created chairman of BNOC and a colourful as well as forceful former chairman of the Courtaulds group, and Mr. Anthony Wedgwood Benn, who had switched jobs at the Department of Industry with Mr. Eric Varley. More experienced heads in the Department of Energy were already pressing for a change of tactics and this accorded both with Lord Kearton's view that the emphasis on financial transactions was wrong and with the Treasury's growing concern about the size of public expenditure.

The result was a change in tactics away from the financial formula originally developed to a simpler offer that the BNOC should agree to purchase 51 per cent of the oil output from fields at market price, thus ensuring the no loss part of the offer, and should gain as eat on the operating board. In the initial stages it might agree to sell a proportion of that oil back. As Lord Kearton argued at the time, thus would the country gain what it needed—control of oil flows for the 1980s when energy might once more be in short supply and a voice in the activities of the oil companies in the meantime while the companies would gain their objective. With Mr. Wedgwood Benn, a supreme negotiator, in the saddle, pressure was immediately brought to bear on BP, whose position was weakened by the 21 per cent of its shares which the Bank of England had taken in return for rescuing Burmah and which BP badly wanted sold back to private shareholders. BP finally agreed in principle, with some adjustments to allow it to take all the North Sea oil early on as long as it ensured a supply in return of Middle East oils. Conoco and Gulf, whose partnership with the National Coal Board meant that they had to give up rather less equity to ensure a 51 per cent state shareholding in the group, followed suit.

Yet Shell, Esso (Exxon as the group is now called) and others—the most important companies in many ways—still remained obdurate, partly for the perfectly good reason that, for them the access to oil was the most important factor in the whole equation. The broader background was getting tense for the Government, as the Treasury placed increasing reliance on the North Sea potential oil flows and on American favour in order to raise its large international loans to finance its budget deficit and the continuing deficits on the balance of payments. And so the approach was changed once more to one of assuring the companies that the oil would be sold back to them although the Government in return would have a right of supervision over the whole of the groups' oil flows, not merely the stated 51 per cent.[10]

It was this offer which Shell and Esso, who had so long set their public face firmly against voluntary participation, finally agreed to in early 1977, spurred partly by the stick of being refused new licences and partly by the feeling that it was an offer which was hardly likely to be improved over time. And it is this offer which is expected to form the basis of the settlements with most of the other remaining companies.

While all this negotiation was going on, however, development of the North Sea was slowing down. Successful oil well tests continued to be announced with regularity throughout 1974/1975/1976. Around a dozen new fields were named and the Government was able to argue voluably that things were getting better rather than worse. The reality was rather different. Although new fields were added to the roster, none were in the "giant" class, less than half could be considered genuinely commercial discoveries in the sense of justifying early development and only one or two, such as Mesa's Beatrice find in the Moray Firth in 1976, could be held to add anything significantly new to previous expectations. The rate of exploration meanwhile declined steadily, though sustained partly by well commitments and partly by a surplus of rigs.

More important, the announcement of new production projects virtually ground to a halt for two years between the end of 1974 and the end of 1976. While existing development programmes continued to suffer delays, there were no further platform orders. Platform construction facilities in Scotland, built-up partly with Government money, faced a bleak prospect of lay-offs if not closure as they came to the end of their work. The total volume of new orders declined in 1976 despite inflation and, although British industry increased its share of orders to over 50 per cent, the atmosphere seemed increasingly one of stagnation as companies re-

---

[10] The Shell and Exxon agreements, signed in a memorandum of January 1977, immediately gave rise to a prolonged, and largely fruitless, public argument as to who had been the victor. What is clear is that there are distinct differences between the BP agreement, which gives the company limited rights of buy-back and requires it to substitute other oils for any North Sea oil it purchases, and the Shell/Exxon agreement, which gives the companies longer rights of buy back and strictly confines BNOC's rights of intervention in development and operating decisions but gives BNOC wider information as to the companies' practice in disposing the oil.

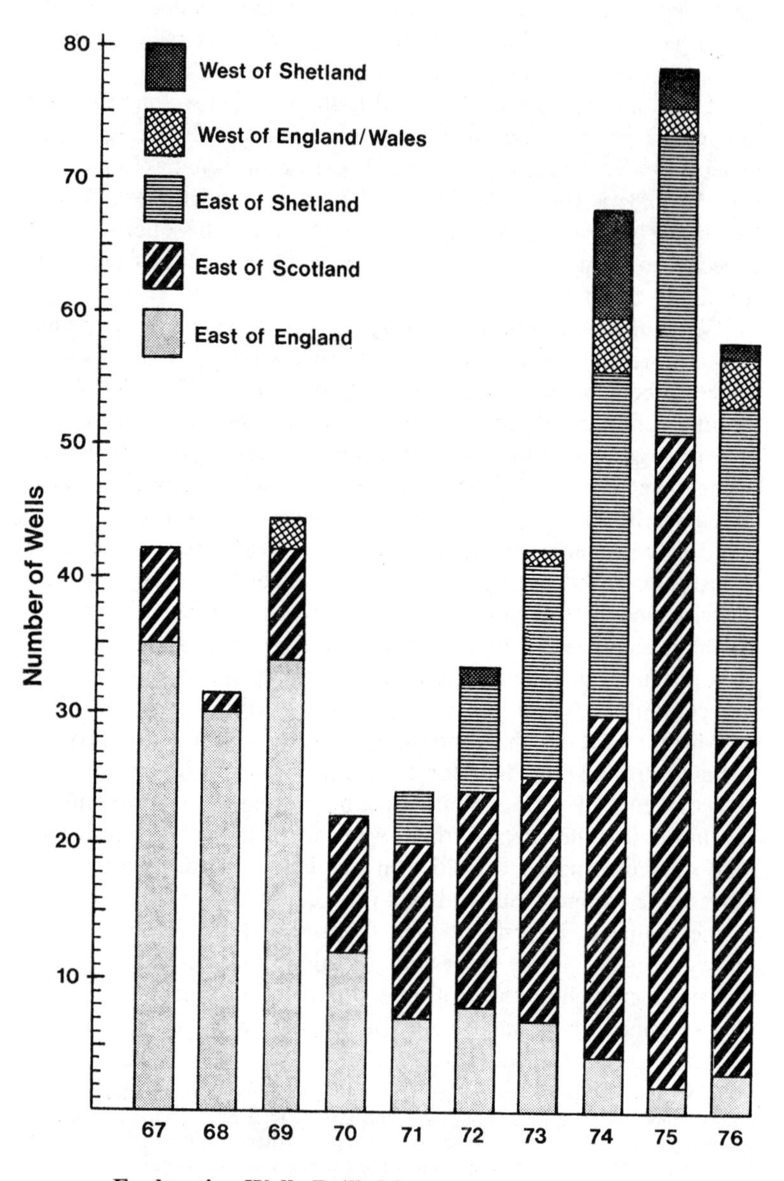

Exploration Wells Drilled in UK Sector 1967-1976

Source: Department of Energy, Brown Book, April 1977.

examined their production plans and industry faced a tailing-off in orders at the very time its general market declined through the worst recession since the 1930s.

How far the political and financial uncertainties induced by Government policies were responsible for this pause has been the subject of one of those endless and tedious political debates on the lines of "it's not my fault and anyway it's not as bad as it seems." Political uncertainties were not the only cause. Oil company problems with digesting what they had already found; uncertainties over the future price of oil; financial caution by the banks facing the consequences of over extending themselves earlier on; engineering problems of producing from the North Sea; the classic cycle of moderating exploration success; the worries over profit and investment amongst even the largest oil companies could all be held to have played a part. But the political problems hardly helped and, on any reasonable assessment, their timing could only have served to further undermine confidence just when it was tottering.

The overriding question left in the wake of these two extraordinary years was not one of who was to blame for what but where was the country to go next. The achievement of the three central planks of Government policy—taxation, control and participation—was intrinsically a reaction to past events rather than a positive approach to the future. Both in the manner and in the aim of the negotiations, the object was to recover from what was felt to be past mistakes.

With the benefit of a series of major oil discoveries, all under development, and with a downgrading of estimates on future energy requirements, a reconsideration may well have been desirable and was certainly possible (if demand had continued to grow at the pre-crisis pace and oil prices had not risen to the extent that they did, then the country would have found itself in a very serious situation indeed).

The question not answered by the various measures taken by the British Government is how it is to use all the powers it had now taken unto itself. If it can now control depletion, does it want to restrict production rates? Should it be taking action to encourage an acceleration in exploration or should it be satisfied to let it go on as it is? Should it force the pace of on-shore related investment, particularly in petrochemicals, or should it leave it to the market? Can it count on a considerable additional reserves being discovered, especially in the newer licenced territories off the west coast, or can it not? Does it matter now that oil is beginning to come ashore in sizeable quantities sufficient to meet internal needs by the end of the decade?

The period 1974-7 has proved a watershed in the development of the North Sea both in the political sense and in the sense that exploration is moving from the primary stage of large fields to the secondary stage of smaller reserve additions. But the real implications of this second stage are only just now being considered.

3 How Much is There

The first question in any assessment of the potential economic value of a raw material, or of the political policy adopted towards its development, is the size of the basic resource itself. And it is here that the uncertainties in oil and gas development become apparent.

For all the increasing sophistication in seismic techniques for mapping out the horizons and possible structures beneath the ground and for all the knowledge that can be gained from outcrops of rock above the ground, only drilling can tell whether and where oil or gas might exist in an area. Even when wells are drilled and the information from them can be correlated with the seismic results to give a more precise picture of the likely traps and conditions, there can still be no certainty that new prospects will not emerge from different horizons or from different traps.[1]

NAM's enormous Groningen find on-shore Holland, which set off the whole search in the southern sector of the North Sea, was itself a surprise after more than a decade of drilling and the completion of some 200 wells by the group. When drilling started in the North Sea there was general expectation that the Dutch sector would be more exciting than the U.K. sector and even within the U.K. sector there were many companies in the industry which felt that the best prospects were in the Mid-North Sea High feature off Yorkshire. In the event the major gas finds were in the southern part of the Basin off Norfolk, and the English sector has so far proved much more prolific than the Dutch side.

North Sea oil, of course, has proved the biggest surprise of all. Within the space of barely four years after the first finds in the northern water off Scotland and Norway in 1969, it was proved to

---

[1] During the early 1970s the oil industry became excited by the prospect that closer seismic definition could record the presence of oil or gas in the so-called "bright spot" technique. While the system has been used in the Gulf of Mexico, however, it requires a relatively clear and simple alignment of different rock strata as well as shallow sediments and has not proved of great value in the North Sea.

be one of the most important and prolific new oil provinces to be established since the War with a potential size equivalent to the proven reserves of Libya or Abu Dhabi and twice the size of those of Venezuela and Nigeria. As the peak period of discoveries has tended to pass, so the inevitable question has been raised about how much more oil can be expected both within the North Sea and in the newer areas of exploration off the western coasts of the North Sea, in the English Channel and towards the far north. Some, particularly amongst the major oil companies, have argued that the ultimate reserves are becoming clearer and that as much as two-thirds of the oil, at least in the U.K. sector of the North Sea, may have already been found. Others, most notably Professor Peter Odell of Erasmus University in Rotterdam, have argued that the oil companies have always tended to be over-conservative and that the ultimate figures could be as much as three times the figures suggested.[2]

The problem really starts with the nature of oil accumulation itself, and the uneven way that oil reserves are spread across the world. Contrary to public belief, oil and gas are found across wide regions on both land and on the Continental Shelves surrounding the present land masses. What is usually missing is not hydrocarbon traces as such but the combination of circumstances necessary to bring it together in sufficient quantities and concentration to make commercial exploitation worthwhile.

To start with, the geological history has to be right for the generation of large volumes of oil. Even on this subject there is uncertainty about how oil is generated. The accepted opinion is that it is created by the decay of marine organisms in the sands or shales of delta or coastal regions millions of years ago. But this is not always true. In the Groningen and the southern North Sea gas fields, the gas appears to have come from ancient coal seams, themselves freshwater deposits, which seeped up into the sandstones deposited later—a picture which helps explain the re-evaluation

---

[2] *The North Sea Oil Province—An Attempt to Simulate Its Development and Exploitation, 1969-2029*, by Peter Odell and Kenneth Rosing (Kogan Page, 1975) For the geology of the North Sea, see the seminal proceedings of a joint Institute of Petroleum conference on *Petroleum and the Continental Shelf of Northwest Europe* held in London in November 1974 (published by Applied Science Publishers, 1975); R. M. Pegrum, G. Rees, S. N. Mounteney and D. Naylor's two-volume *Geology of the North-West European Continental Shelf* (Graham Trotman Dudley, 1975); and E. N. Tiratsoo's *Oilfields of the World* (Scientific Press, 1973).

which followed the Groningen discovery as many oil companies had previously expected oil and gas to be found only in the younger Mesozoic and Tertiary rocks which account for more than 90 per cent of the world's oil and three-quarters of its gas.

Once the oil has been generated, then the conditions have to be right for it to migrate from a wide area into suitable reservoir rocks —sandstone or limestone—in which it can be accumulated and flow in the tiny interconnecting pores between the grains. And for this to happen, there has to be the right trapping mechanism such as a dome or fault in which the reservoir rock is overlain with a cap rock of impermeable material through which the oil and gas cannot escape. If the reservoir rock is too heavily compressed by the weight of rocks above, there will not be enough pore spaces for it to accumulate in sufficient quantities nor might there be sufficient interconnection between spaces for the oil to flow through the rock upwards when a well is drilled. If the structure is not there, then it will be spread across too wide an area. If the cap rock is broken, it will escape.

It is the establishment of this combination of circumstances which is so difficult during the early years of exploration and which requires the drilling of wells to confirm.

The first major find in the North Sea, by the Phillips group at Ekofisk off Norway, was found in fractured Danian and Upper Cretaceous chalk, both relatively unusual circumstances for a good oil field (since oil does not flow easily through chalk unless it has been heavily fractured by later movements in the rocks above) and in a situation localised in this part of the North Sea.

Even when this find had shown that large oil fields could exist, the first thought among much of the oil industry on the U.K. side was to look for structures in the Tertiary rocks, where Amoco found the Montrose Field at around the same time and BP found the Forties Field a year later. With this in mind it was these potential structures which aroused most interest in the fourth round of licences. Yet it was the Jurassic structures in the quite different circumstances of the highly productive trough east of the Shetlands —where the oil was trapped in tilted blocks beneath an unconformity which made seismic reading difficult for a long time—that most of the oil has been found since. And if Shell-Esso first gained a handle on this geological play with its Brent discovery of 1971, its experience in bidding £21m. for a single block and its failure to find an oil field on it showed the vagaries of exploration.

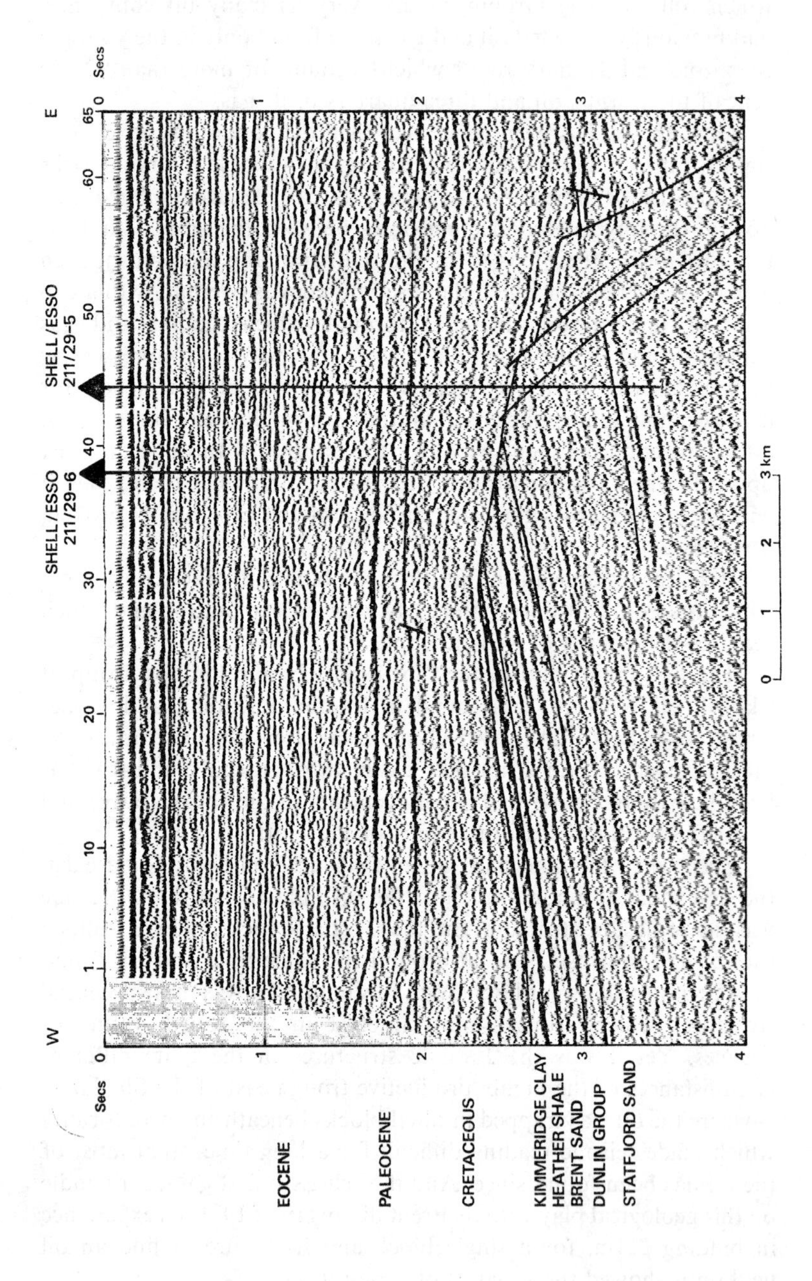
W
E
Secs
SHELL/ESSO
211/29-6
SHELL/ESSO
211/29-5
EOCENE
PALEOCENE
CRETACEOUS
KIMMERIDGE CLAY
HEATHER SHALE
BRENT SAND
DUNLIN GROUP
STATFJORD SAND
3 km

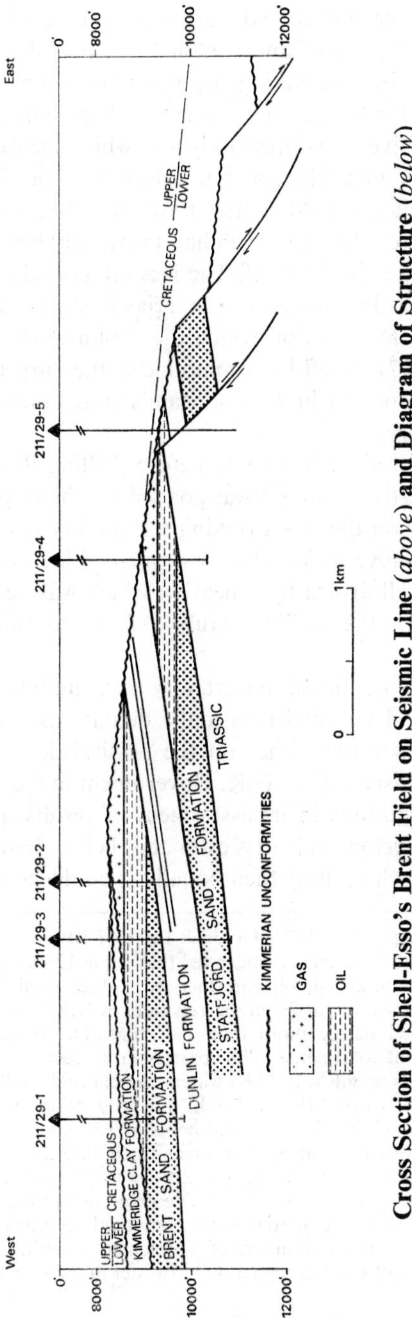

Cross Section of Shell-Esso's Brent Field on Seismic Line *(above)* **and Diagram of Structure** *(below)*

North Sea Impact

Such uncertainties and surprises can occur even late in the exploration history of an area. In 1976, the Mesa group surprised the industry by discovering a potentially commercial field just off the Moray Firth coast in a region where half-a-dozen wells had been drilled five years previously and which the industry had tended to give up as unexciting. A year before, the Gas Corporation found an important gas field in the East Irish Sea Basin off Liverpool extending into a licence which had previously been drilled and given up as unproductive by Gulf. The Hewett gas field was discovered by the Arpet and Phillips groups in Triassic strata much younger than the Permian horizons on which the exploration effort was concentrated. In 1977, Shell-Esso announced the surprise discovery of a sizeable oil column in Jurassic sands (the Fulmar find) next to its Auk discovery.

BP itself waited five years before drilling its Forties Field and only then partly because it was goaded by Shell's persistent attempts to "farm in" on the block (taking a share in exchange for doing the drilling)—a move which Shell had pursued because of the results of a previous well drilled by it nearby, which was never tested because its partner in the drilling, Gulf, refused to fund the additional expense.

With this continual uncertainty surrounding exploration, any country would be unwise to make definite assumptions about the size of its resources, either on the pessimistic or, for that matter, the optimistic side. If the U.K. Government in the early years proved excessively cautious in its assessment of results, publishing reserve figures well below industry estimates being made at the time by companies such as BP,[3] then equally it could be said that the U.S.

[3] As early as September 1972, Dr. Jack Birks of BP, in a speech to a *Financial Times* North Sea Conference, suggested that some 12bn. barrels of commercial, and possibly commercial, oil had then been discovered in all sectors of the North Sea of which about 7·5bn. barrels were in U.K.waters when Government figures suggested barely more than half that. Dr. Birks suggested national assessment might total some 47bn. barrels in all sectors of the North Sea, of which two-thirds might be in U.K. waters. A year and a half later, in May 1974, the Government's first "Brown Book" on production and reserves, suggested that reserves in existing finds totalled between 9·5bn. and 11bn. barrels and that probable reserves from all existing areas (including the licensed areas west of the U.K. as well as the North Sea) might rise to 14·7bn. with a possible total of 21bn. BP has broadly kept to its ultimate projections since, with a slight downgrading of the U.K.'s potential share compared to Norway's. In an amusing sidelight on the political influence of government on ministry reports, however, the appointment of Lord Balogh as Oil Minister in the new Labour Government

(*continued on page 53*)

Government (and to some extent Iran) has proved notoriously reluctant to accept until late in the day the reality of its steady decline in both gas and oil reserves, for all the optimistic noises of future potential made by the U.S. Government sponsored geological survey in recent years (which have tended to come down of late) and the increase in exploration investment which followed the 1973/4 crisis.

What can be said is that the history of exploration, particularly in well-established oil provinces such as the U.S., Canada and Iran, has been one of a series of gradual phases, starting with initial failure as companies have tried to interpret the geology; spurting as the first big finds are made and the knowledge of a succession of wells enables the industry as a whole to define its target more closely; beginning to ease off as most of the larger structures are tested and exploration turns to the smaller possibilities nearby or the more delicate structures (such as stratigraphic traps caused by changes in the nature of the rocks difficult to see on the seismic picture); followed by a secondary phase as production experience improves, smaller finds are brought in and the development settles in to a long-term pattern of development.

These phases can be sharpened by Government action or outside events. In the North Sea, the Government's licencing policy rapidly accelerated the speed at which oil reserves were proved in the North Sea between 1971 and 1973. Government policy could equally sharpen the rate at which exploration falls off, as it did in the southern sector of the North Sea over the period 1969-1971 and in the northern area in 1975 and 1976. The phases can also be distorted by the ever-present fact that it is the giant discoveries of 1bn. barrels or more which change the face of exploration.

But under normal conditions, the phases tend to be much less sharp than oil industry statements would suggest. The exploration industry, like any other industry, tends to promote an emotional

[3] (*continued from page 52*)
of 1974 resulted in a dramatic re-appraisal in the following year, when the "Brown Book" added in an estimate of a possible 11bn. barrels of ultimate reserves in designated areas not yet licensed to make an ultimate possible total in U.K. waters of 33bn. barrels. At that time the designated areas did not include the Western Approaches or the area to Rockall. The ultimate figure has more recently been kept at between 22bn. and 33bn. barrels and, in the most recent "Brown Book", (April 1977) it was stressed that "the higher end of the range now includes an allowance for areas not yet designated but expected to fall to the U.K. when the dividing line between the U.K. and other countries such as France, Norway and Ireland are fully determined".

concensus in reaction to events. When the first big discoveries are made, there is an atmosphere of limitless possibility (in the early stages of gas discoveries estimates for Leman Bank and other fields were made that proved over-optimistic in the event just as Ekofisk was later to bring suggestions by some of the partner companies that Europe might become self-sufficient in oil over a short time). When the period of large discoveries seems to be over, companies tend to grow too conservative all at once.

In the event, history elsewhere suggests that the secondary phase of exploration tends to be rather more successful and prolonged than at first thought as companies upgrade reserves in existing fields and find numerous smaller features that can be tied in around the major finds and as the productivity and life of fields exceeds initial estimates. This tendency in turn has given rise to the argument, put most forcefully by Professor Odell, that companies are innately conservative in their official reserve calculations and that, on the basis of experience in North America, a continuous process of upgrading on a sizeable scale can be expected during the history of an oil province.

Professor Odell's view has been sharply challenged by the oil companies on the grounds that the North Sea history cannot be compared to that of Canada or the U.S. In the first place the experience of successive re-evaluations of reserves in North America has arisen from the rigid stock exchange and governmental controls which require companies to announce only those reserves which have been fully proved, particularly in Alberta where Government allocations on production encouraged companies to keep pushing up reserves in order to gain more production allowances. In the second place, the requirements of off-shore investment planning are quite different from those on-shore. On land, a company can move step by step with its wells and production facilities, starting at the centre and moving out to gain the cash flow from first production to fund the next facilities (although even this is becoming less true). Off-shore, a company has to make a decision as a whole because of the expense of installing production platforms. And it is hardly in its interests to underestimate reserves by any significant amount lest that leaves it with insufficient capacity on its platforms to cope with the additional production.

Certainly, the history of the Brent and Forties fields is one of initial assessments of reserves being made after only three or four wells, while the experience of fields such as Cormorant and Ninian

Brae and Hutton is of initial overestimates rather than underestimates of reserves.

Yet there is clearly an element of truth in what Professor Odell has argued. The calculation of recoverable reserves is, to an extent, a commercial assessment of what can be recovered, given present technology and costs. While it may be in the interests of the petroleum geologist to push his particular project within a company by proclaiming its virtues, once it comes to the production planning and the formal reserve assessments, the natural tendency must be to leave a margin of error on the topside. Nobody gets into trouble for underestimating, but they do if they overestimate. The official figures for the North Sea, too, have been influenced by the need to present assessments, largely made by outside consultants, for the banks in order to raise finance and this in turn promotes a degree of conservatism. As further drilling is carried out and production is undertaken, there is a tendency for the figures to move up. And this has happened with a number of fields such as Piper (whose official reserves were assessed by consultants for the banks), Brent and Auk (where further drilling in both cases found additional oil reservoirs, in the former case on the eastern edge and in the latter in a producing reservoir deeper down). A substantial re-evaluation of overall reserves in this way seems unlikely and there can be disappointments as well as successes. But it would not be surprising if perhaps 10 or 20 per cent is added to reserve and production estimates of existing fields in time.

The point is important because the effect of the U.K. determination to press ahead with rapid exploration through attractive licensing terms and large licence issues has been to take U.K. off-shore exploration to a much more mature phase than that of its neighbours in North-West Europe and to raise the very real question whether the best has now been found.

Taking the North Sea as a whole, there can now be no question as to the importance of its potential oil reserves not only in terms of its local impact on the surrounding host countries but also in terms of the world oil trade as a whole. Existing discoveries in the presently allocated North Sea, both proven and "probable" (that is potentially commercial but yet to be delineated), by the Spring of 1977 approached 25 billion barrels of recoverable oil and around 90 trillion cubic feet of gas. Of these some 60 per cent of the oil was in U.K. waters with the remainder largely lying in the Norwegian sector. The gas reserves are shared as to about two-thirds in the

Oil Fields Under Commercial Development (Aug. 1977)

Field	Operator	Block No.	Dis-covered	Re-serves (*million barrels*)	Produc-tion start-up	Peak Produc-tion (*barrels per day*)
Argyll	Hamilton	30/24	1971	25	1975	27,000
Forties	BP	21/10	1970	1,800	1975	500,000
Auk	Shell	30/16	1970	60	1976	40,000
Beryl	Mobil	9/13	1972	520	1976	80,000
Montrose	Amoco	22/17	1969	150	1976	50,000
Brent	Shell	211/29	1971	2,000	1976	470,000
Piper	Occidental	15/17	1973	800	1976	300,000
Claymore	Occidental	14/19	1974	420	1977	170,000
Dunlin	Shell	211/23+24	1973	600	1978	150,000
Heather	Unocal	2/5	1973	150	1978	50,000
Thistle	BNOC	211/18+19	1973	560	1978	200,000
Ninian	Chevron	3/3+8	1974	1,050	1978	350,000
Cormorant	Shell	211/26	1972	150	1979	60,000
Statfjord (U.K.)	Statoil	211/24	1974	400	1979	70,000
Buchan	BP	21/1	1974	50	1979	50-80,000
Beatrice	Mesa	11/30	1976	170	1979	100,000
Tartan	Texaco	15/16	1974	2-300	1979/80	70-80,000
Murchison	Conoco	211/19	1975	300	1980	90,000

U.K. section, a quarter in Norwegian waters and the remainder in the Dutch sector. About 70 per cent of the gas is in non-associated reserves—that is not part of an oil field.

In terms of production, about 60 per cent of the total discovered oil reserves in all sectors and rather more than a half of the gas reserves are currently being developed or planned for development, suggesting a total oil production from the North Sea of around 3·5-4 million barrels per day by the early 1980s (of which 2·5 million barrels per day might be from the U.K. sector) and 8,500m. cubic feet of gas per day (of which around 5,500m. may be coming from the U.K. sector. Total gas production will be equivalent to 1·3m. barrels per day of oil.

Looking ahead, most estimates would seem to assume that an ultimate total reserve approaching 35-40bn. barrels of oil and around 100-150 trillion cubic feet of gas might eventually be found in all sectors of the North Sea south of the 62nd Parallel. This would put the North Sea in the same reserve category as the U.S. (which currently produces around 10m. barrels per day including gas liquids) and well above the North African countries in terms of oil resources, although rather a smaller proportion of U.S. or world gas reserves. It would also be theoretically sufficient (if the Norwegians let production expand without restrictions) to supply around 30 per cent of Western Europe's expected needs of gas and oil in the 1980s.[4]

Although this assumes a relatively healthy additional discovery of around 50-60 per cent more oil and gas than has already been found, it is by no means certain that the U.K. will continue to hold its existing share of these reserves. With a long coastline, the U.K.

---

[4] Various projections of the ultimate potential of the North Sea have been given. The latest Government estimates (*Development of the oil and gas resources of the United Kingdom*, report to Parliament, April 1977) suggests a probable total of 14·4bn. barrels of oil in existing discoveries and a possible total of 17-24bn. barrels in all currently licensed territory. A possible total of 22-33bn. barrels is given for all areas, including those unlicensed (although without much confidence). Possible gas reserves in existing discoveries is given as 51 trillion cubic feet, of which nearly half are in the southern sector. No estimates of potential reserves are stated. Other estimates have come largely from brokers (Wood, Mackenzie and Co. being the most authoritative), from Professor Colin Robinson's group at the University of Surrey ("World oil prices and the profitability of North Sea oil," *Petroleum Review*, April 1976) and the oil companies. Roger Bexon of BP, in a speech to the *Financial Times'* North Sea conference in October 1974, put ultimate oil reserves in the North Sea at 42bn. barrels, of which 26bn. might be in the U.K. sector, and total ultimate reserves of non-associated gas in all sectors at 109 trillion cubic feet (of which half, again, might be in U.K. territory). Shell's information brief, *Offshore oil and gas, north-west Europe* (July 1976) suggests that ultimately recoverable reserves in the North Sea may total 35bn. barrels of oil and 110-150 trillion cubic feet of which 23bn. barrels of oil and 90 trillion cubic feet of gas (65 trillion cubic feet of which was non-associated) had already been found. Estimates by Mobil and Exxon would broadly fit these projections.

Other Potentially Commercial Oil Discoveries

Field	Block No.	Operator	Discovery	Estimated reserves (*million barrels*)	Possible start-up	Peak production (*barrels per day*)
Magnus	211/12	BP	1974	4-500	1981/2	100,000
Fulmar	30/16	Shell	1975	3-500	1980/1	150,000
Alwyn	3/14+15	Total	1973	2-300	1981/2	100,000
North Cormorant	211/21	Shell	1972	3-400	1981/2	75-150,000
Thelma	16/17	Phillips	1976	2-400	1981/2	100,000
Hutton	211/28+27	Conoco	1973	200	1982/3	50-100,000
North West Hutton	211/27	Amoco	1975	200	1982/4	50-100,000
Tern	210/25	Shell	1975	250-300	early to mid-80s	100,000
—	211/16	Shell	1976	250	early to mid-80s	50-80,000
North Thistle	211/18	BNOC	1976	1-200	1981	50-80,000
North Beryl	9/13	Mobil	1975	200	1981/3	5-70,000
South Brae	16/7	Pan Ocean	1975	2-300	1982/3	70-100,000
South West Ninian	3/7	Chevron	1976	100	early to mid-80s	50-70,00
Maureen	16/29	Phillips	1973	80-120	early to mid-80s	50-70,00
Andrew	16/28	BP	1974	150	early to mid-80s	50-70,000
Lyell	3/2	Conoco	1975	50	mid-80s	30-40,000
Renee	15/27	Phillips	1976	50	mid-80s	30-40,000
Crawford	9/28	Hamilton	1975	1-200 (for these five rows together)		
—	2/10	Siebens	1975			
—	14/20	Texaco	1975			
—	206/28	BP	1977			
—	9/19	Conoco	1976			

Gas Fields Under Commercial Development

Field	Operator	Block No.	Discovered	Reserves (*trillion cubic feet*) Remaining reserves in brackets	Production start-up	Peak average production (*million cubic feet per day*)
West Sole	BP	48/6	1965	2·2 (1·6)	1967	230
Lemon Bank	Shell/Amoco	48/26+ 49/27	1966	10·5 (7·2)	1968	1640
Indefatigable	Amoco/Shell	49/23+ 49/19+24	1966	4·5 (3·3)	1971	740
Hewett	Phillips	48/29+30	1966	3·4 (2·2)	1969	850
Viking	Conoco	49/17+12	1968	4·5 (3·6)	1972	700
Rough	Amoco	49/17	1968	0·5 (0·4)	1975	150
Frigg (U.K.)	Total	10/1	1972	3·0	1977	600
Frent (assoc gas)	Shell	211/29	1971	3·0	1980	600

has been fortunate in the amount of territory it has gained from the division of the North Sea. Of the 200,000 square miles of the North Sea south of the 62nd Parallel, the U.K. has been able to claim around 95,000 square miles or more than 46 per cent. Further north, however, it is Norway, which has the largest Continental Shelf area in Europe and six times as much territory north of the 62nd Parallel as south of it (and it has only allocated about 20 per cent of its territory south of the 62nd). It is this area, and that off the eastern part of Greenland, which is generally held to be one of the most potentially important unexplored basins in the world.

Within currently licensed territory, in the North Sea, the U.K. again seems to have been relatively fortunate as most of the potentially productive sedimentary basins in both the southern North Sea Basin and in the complex of troughs off Scotland and the Shetlands lie in its territory. But it is an area which has very largely been licensed already with most of the few outstanding blocks left out of

Other Potentially Commercial Gas Fields

Field	Block No.	Operator	Discovered	Estimated reserves (*trillion cubic feet*)
Morecambe Bay	110/2	British Gas	1974	3-3·5
Amethyst	47/14	Burmah	1972	0·5
Audrey	49/11	Phillips	1976	2·0
Sean	49/25	Shell	1969	1-2
Deborah	48/30	Phillips	1968	0·5
Ann	49/6	Phillips	1966	0·3–0·5
Broken Bank	49/16	Conoco	1970	—
—	48/12	Transocean	1975	1·0
—	3/25	Total	1974	—

Condensate Discoveries

Field	Block No.	Operator	Discovered
Lomond	23/21	Amoco	1972
Bruce	9/8	Hamilton	1974
North Brae	16/7	Pan Ocean	1975
—	21/2	Zapata	1975
—	211/13	Shell/Esso	1974
—	15/30	Conoco	1975
—	30/2	BNOC	1971

Source: Department of Energy, Wood, Mackenzie and industry

the fourth round now allocated in the fifth) and extensively explored. Of the 800 or so exploration and appraisal wells drilled in all sectors of the North Sea by the end of 1976, more than 600 were in U.K. territory, with the proportion swinging dramatically in favour of northern waters.

In spite of persistent Government declarations that exploration rates continue as high as ever and that the rate of discovery is improving rather than diminishing (24 claimed "significant" oil finds and four gas finds in 1975 followed by a dozen oil finds and two gas finds in 1976), closer examination of the quality and size of the finds suggests that the pace of "wildcatting" (pure exploration) is going down and that the rate of discovery of additional reserves is falling.

Compared to a peak exploration activity in U.K. waters of over 300 "string months" in 1975, 1976 saw a fall to 269 while 1977 is expected to see 234, of which a high proportion is likely to be wells drilled to appraise existing finds rather than test totally new traps. The list of new finds, while looking impressive, is rather less sensational when potential reserves and commercial prospects are considered. A number of them have been finds made in ancillary structure to the main fields (such as the proving of the U.K. extension to the giant Norwegian Statfjord find and the discoveries around Ninian, Brent and Beryl). Of the discoveries made in the period 1975-6, only around half-a-dozen could be called "significant" in the sense of being strong candidates for early development—including Tern, Murchison, Beatrice, Fulmer and possibly Brae and Thelma. Of these, only Beatrice and Fulmer had really opened up new geological possibilities.

This is not to downgrade the results of recent finds. That some may have been made in the area of major fields under development suggests they can form useful additional reserves that may be tied in to the producing facilities on the main fields. Even if fairly small in individual size, a number could be developed over a short time span using floating production facilities connected to subsea completions (as already used on the Argyll Field and planned for Buchan). As their numbers increase, so the longer-term possibilities of group developments rise.

But it does mean that the industry is having to work increasingly hard to add sizeable new reserves to the U.K. total as it comes across smaller accumulations of oil and as the pace of discovery gradually eases off. Of the 14-16bn. barrels of oil so far established in the U.K. North Sea, 9bn. are in the 18 fields already under development and a third of total reserves are accounted for by just three fields (Brent, Ninian and Forties), leaving around 5bn. barrels of reserves not committed to production scattered around in about three dozen finds with reserves of anything between 20 to 500m. barrels of recoverable oil. And the same picture is probably true of gas, although the estimates are more difficult because of the potential quantities of gas associated with oil. Of the 35-40 trillion cubic feet of natural gas already discovered, some 25 trillion are in fields already under development and committed to the Gas Corporation, while as much as half of the non-committed gas lies in association with oil in fields all around the northern waters.

Looking to future possibilities, there is no reason to believe that substantial quantities of additional oil and gas will not be found in the U.K. North Sea. Indeed the history of other exploration areas is that the phase of numerous but smaller reserve additions tends to last longer than the industry would sometimes proclaim. But the ultimate figure would seem to be more and more clearly in view. The main pattern of North Sea troughs in which the oil finds have been made has now been relatively well covered with exploration drilling.

In the southern sector of the North Sea, and most productive gas province, exploration has undoubtedly been affected by the low price paid for gas and the indications that the gas industry has little wish for further supplies from this area until the main fields go into decline in the early eighties. A further 3 trillion cubic feet has already been discovered in small accumulations around the Leman Bank, Indefatigable and Hewett areas. Given the price incentive to boost exploration, further additions of a few million cubic feet might be expected. But, at this stage, it looks unlikely that very much more can be anticipated.

In the northern North Sea, the most important area of oil discoveries, the relatively narrow, highly productive, Viking Graben, which stretches north-south east of the Shetlands, is now fairly well explored. Drilling in deeper waters just below the 62nd Parallel at the edge of the Shelf and exploration of the prospects of accumulations against the Platform on the western side of the graben have both proved disappointing. The major structures are in tilted fault blocks so that a good deal of drilling will be required to explore fully the possibilities of additional finds around the main fields. Although a number of new finds can be expected, the chances of any major field with reserves of 500m. or more barrels seem limited. Further south, at the neck of the trough, potentially sizeable quantities of oil and gas have been found in Brae and Thelma against a "high" feature, but the quality of the Jurassic sands in the area tends to be variable, and the elongated structures will not be easy to develop (unfortunately the oil does not seem to have accumulated right up against the High).

The complex area of the Forties Trough and Moray Firth Basin off the coast of the Scottish mainland and the Orkneys has presented more varied conditions. Forties continues to be the only giant field discovered so far there. But the Piper discovery off the Moray Firth has set off a series of successful exploration efforts in the Jurassic horizons in the area and promoted considerable interest in the blocks once thought less interesting and now allocated in the fifth round of licensing. More recently, the Mesa find of the Beatrice field close to the Moray Firth shore in middle Jurassic sands has proved a real surprise, although prospects for further finds in this part are somewhat diminished by the degree of geological upheaval and lack of structures. An interesting condensate[5] and gas "play" has developed around the southern part of sector 15 in cretacious rocks, although the conditions are fairly localised. The Buchan Field has been found in Devonian sandstones of much older age than other North Sea finds (the oil appears to have migrated from the younger rocks), although again this type of find presents problems of reservoir condition. Shell has caused a re-evaluation of the central North Sea area with its Jurassic Fulmer discovery next to Auk.[6] Added to this there have been finds of both oil, gas and condensate further towards the median line with the Norwegian sector.

---

[5] "Condensate" is the term used to describe liquid hydrocarbons with low specific gravity which separate from gas at surface conditions. Although used extensively in the U.S. as a petrochemical feedstock, their production presents considerable technical as well as economic difficulties, particularly in pipelining to the shore. There are now a number of interesting condensate discoveries in the U.K. North Sea (including Hamilton Brothers' Bruce and Crawford Fields, Amoco's Lomond Field as well as the discoveries in sectors 15). But it is doubtful, at this stage, whether they are large or concentrated enough to justify a transportation system however. Small quantities of condensate are already being produced from the main oil fields and more will be expected from the northern gas or associated gas reserves, Williams-Merz's study of potential gas gathering pipeline systems, published by the Department of Energy in May 1976, discusses some of the potential production possibilities and problems. But so far there has been no detailed assessment of potential reserves.

[6] (*See page 64.*)

It is a reasonably long odds bet that at least one more giant oil field will be found in the North Sea. It is an even better bet that a number of further commercial discoveries will be made. But the drilling of the last two years does, for the moment, seem to support the growing consensus in the industry and the Government that ultimate reserves of oil in the U.K. sector of the North Sea will probably be around 20-25bn. barrels, implying both that two-thirds may have already been discovered and that considerable further effort will have to be made if the remaining 5-10bn. barrels are to be found.

In the newer areas off the western coasts of the U.K., exploration is still at the stage which the North Sea was before the Ekofisk and Forties Field discoveries. The geological history is quite different from the Trough-system of the North Sea. Many of the best prospects are in very deep water of 1,000 feet and more. Oil has already been proved to have been generated, but none of the surveys and the drilling so far carried out has shown whether the conditions of generation and trapping are right for substantial reserves.

There are two major basin areas, one to the far north extending west of the Shetlands and ultimately out to the basins around the Faroes and Rockall; and the other to the south, the so-called Western Approaches Basin, extending south-west from Cornwall and Devon out to the south-west of Ireland and north-west of Brittany.

Allocations in the West Shetlands area (really a complex of basins) were made in the fourth round and, by the summer of 1977, some 16 wells had been drilled, mostly in the Inner Basin closest to the Shetlands and on the Median, or Ridge Edge of the Continental Shelf separating the inner basin from the deep outer basin extending down the Continental Slope to the Faroes-Shetland tertiary basinal channel which is in very deep water.

The drilling results so far have been mixed. The first dozen wells in the Inner Basin and on the Ridge were extremely disappointing, although Shell found some traces of oil in one of its first wells. More recently, however, BP has announced (in July 1977) the discovery of a sizeable oil column in a shallow well drilled on the

---

[6] Shell's Fulmar discovery—made in 1976 and kept quiet until a second well was drilled in the Spring of 1977—was unexpected, mainly because of the size of the oil column encountered (believed to be around 600 ft.). The presence of oil in Jurassic sands in this area was already known from Hamilton Brothers' drilling on the Argyll Field and a nearby well drilled by Phillips. But these showed only traces of oil. The Shell discovery has caused some rethinking in the industry but it remains to be seen whether it will lead to a radical revision of potential oil estimates in this part of the North Sea.

Ridge in the north-western part of the area (block 206/8) whilst Shell, in a joint well with Total on block 206/5 drilled on the outer side of the Ridge nearby in 1976, is also believed to have encountered interesting evidence of oil.

The BP find, less than 50 miles from the shore in 450 feet of water, was of heavy oil and the flow rates were far from encouraging for a commercial discovery in itself. But the results, and more particularly those of the Shell find, at least give rise to the hope that there may be a localised oil basin in the north-west part of currently licensed acreage. More important, they suggest some potential further out towards the Faroes over the edge of the Continental Shelf, where the Tertiary deposits thicken dramatically and where the possibilities of oil generation are held to be good. Broad seismic surveys have not suggested a great many large structures. The area, currently unlicensed, is in very deep water indeed and companies at this time are not looking for early exploration and production from such depths. One guess as to reserve potential plucked out of the air by an experienced geologist suggested 4bn. barrels. This is very much a stab in the dark but at least the BP and Shell finds suggest a long-term prospect of interest.

A similar evaluation could at the moment be made of the possibilities in the Western Approaches. So far the only drilling has been carried out in a few wells on the French side nearer in to the Brittany coast. Some oil traces have been found but have not given great encouragement to the industry. Agreement on a median line between France and Britain in the summer of 1977 has given new impetus to exploration, particularly as the Government is now considering offering licences in the area during 1978. Seismic surveys have suggested considerable depths of Mesozoic and Tertiary sediments and some big structures. Again there are not a large number of structures and the best prospects seem to be out in deep water further from the coast, so that the economics of production will demand large finds. But as a long-term prospect for Britain, it remains attractive, if unknown.

Between these two longer-term prospects north-west and south-west of Britain lie a number of smaller basins off the west coast of Scotland and Wales which are unlikely to hold major reserves but which could provide useful finds closer to shore. BP, having returned its licences in the Minch Basin between the mainland coast of Scotland and the Hebrides, has taken out in the fifth round a couple of highly speculative blocks to the west of the Hebrides. In the Manx-Furness, or East Irish Sea, Basin off Morecambe Bay the Gas Corporation has made a useful discovery of gas with reserves of more than 3 trillion cubic feet on territory partly relinquished by Gulf (which had already drilled a well there but failed to test it fully). Work by Amoco further west, however, suggests that the Basin could hold little else.

In Cardigan Bay, a number of new licences have been taken out in the fifth round in what is really an extension of the North Celtic Sea Basin south of Ireland. While both gas and oil traces have been found off Cork in Irish territory (in Cretaceous strata), the evidence there does not suggest large fields and enthusiasm for British prospects is not high. Nor, after two disappointing wells by Shell and BP, is there much optimism about the South Celtic Sea Basin north of Devon off south-west Wales. Under existing well commitment, further drilling will have to be undertaken but, for the present, there seems a general propensity to return acreage.

In the English Channel, meanwhile, the discovery by the Gas Corporation of a commercial on-shore oil field in Jurassic sands at Wych Farm in Dorset has aroused some interest in the off-shore prospects, where the Jurassic sands thicken. One or two large structures have been shown up on seismic surveys. They are few and the difficulties of producing oil from one of the world's busiest shipping lanes are daunting.

With the passing of the exploration peak in the North Sea, therefore, the U.K. is at an intriguing point so far as its resources are concerned. For the moment she has enough discovered reserves to assure herself of oil sufficiency through much of the next decade, although she will need to ensure production from some of the smaller fields if she is to achieve this through the eighties.

Over the medium-term there seems a chance that she may increase her oil and gas reserves in the North Sea by as much as 50 per cent provided that the exploration momentum is there. For the much longer-term, there is the possibility—some exploration geologists would regard it as quite a reasonable possibility—that significant new reserves may be found in the deeper basins west of the Shetlands and in the South-Western Approaches, although these are unlikely to be as productive as the North Sea.

Neither of these prospects are in any way certain. Before the Government can decide whether it needs, or wants, to gear up development over the medium-term, it really needs to know how good are its prospects for the longer-term. Yet this in turn must raise questions not only as to its licensing policy (which, at the moment, seems to have developed into one of regular small allocations) but also towards the role of BNOC, whose natural instincts will be to go for the obvious rather than the speculative blocks, and towards exploration competition, which in turn may be reduced by the presence of BNOC and the natural preference of both the Corporation and the civil service for the multi-national companies rather than the independent exploration groups.

4 The Pace of Development

While the fundamental factor governing the timing, size and pace of development off-shore must remain the vagaries of exploration success itself, attention in the last few years has turned more and more from the search for oil to the costs and benefits of getting into production.

As with exploration, the estimates have tended to veer dramatically from initial optimism to sudden pessimism and back to renewed optimism as the oil industry, first, announced its initial production plans, then encountered the problems of delays, cost escalation and profit re-assessment, and then overcome these in a more ebullient mood as the oil has finally started to flow and production performance has, in some cases, outstripped first expectations. Initial projections made in late 1973 had suggested that total North Sea oil production would start in late 1974 and build up to as much as 3m. barrels per day in 1980 and—according to some—over 4m. barrels per day in the mid-eighties. Within a year the difficulties encountered in development had forced a postponement of the year of start-up until 1975 and a general shaving-down of production estimates for the following years by as much as a quarter to a third. Without a price rise of substantial proportions and with continued demand growth along pre-crisis trends, the North Sea and the country would have been in serious difficulties.

Now, with a price rise, with much lower growth of demand, and with a general optimism drawn from initial production rates, confidence that targets of self-sufficiency can be reached has returned. However, the effects of the delay of two years in new field developments and the continued uncertainties over future price trends and demand curves have left a number of questions overhanging the likely course of oil production through the eighties and into the nineties.

Much of the difficulty of assessing accurately the output curve of off-shore oil (and gas) over the medium and long term arises from the nature of North Sea production. A considerable amount has been written about the problems and technical challenge involved in producing oil and gas from the waters off Scotland. The storms encountered there are not necessarily worse than the typhoons of the Gulf of Mexico. The water depths are not as great as those tackled in the drilling which has been going on off Eastern Canada. Nor are the average conditions or logistical problems any worse than those in Alaska or Greenland.

But the North Sea is unique in the consistency of pressures that the sea exerts on production platforms, the average height of the waves, the unpredictability of the weather and the proportion of the year in which supply and installation work can be made impossible by sea and weather conditions. The North Sea also presents problems in that, with a few exceptions, almost all the fields have been found in water of over 300 feet in depth around 100 miles or more from shore, while the majority of them lie nearer the islands of the Orkneys and Shetlands than the mainland.

These conditions produce a number of important problems for development, and help to explain the sudden deceleration in new development plans in the North Sea.

One is that production planning for a field has to be undertaken as a single plan for the whole field, very often from limited reservoir knowledge. On land it is possible to develop a field in phases, to drill a more extensive pattern of wells before determining final reserves and to test individual wells over a prolonged period before assessing flow characteristics. Off-shore, because of the cost of drilling and the limitations of equipment on a rig, the assessment has to be made from only a few wells and the production tests tend to be more limited than those made on land.

Once again, this has given rise to the feeling that the oil companies are far too conservative in their initial announcements and that production tends to be better than was at first thought. This must be partly true. It is not in the interests of petroleum engineers to lean towards over-optimism in their assessments of productivity. The case of Forties and Piper in the winter of 1976/7, when initial flow rates proved much better than predicted, would seem to support this interpretation.

There remains the risk on the other side, however, particularly in fields where reservoirs lie in limestone or chalk, where production is dependent on fractures or tightly compacted sandstones. The on-shore Lockton gas field was developed in the mid-sixties at considerable expense and contracted to the Gas Corporation, only for the producing company, Home Oil, to find that the wells in

Zechstein strata failed to maintain the initial high flow rates. The pressures declined, water encroached and the reserves had to be completely devalued. The Argyll Field off Edinburgh, the first field into production, experienced substantial water encroachment in the Spring of 1977 and may not last beyond 1979. The peak flow rates—although not the ultimate reserves—from the Groningen Field have recently been devalued by 20 per cent, causing a considerable degree of anguished re-assessment by the Dutch Government which had encouraged an extensive commitment of gas in export contracts. Early in 1976, the Norwegian authorities re-assessed the reserves and production from the Ekofisk Field and a similar devaluation of its expected production. Development of the Dan Field off Denmark has proved a costly and prolonged process of re-evaluation of productivity.[1]

Most of the U.K. North Sea fields under development are in younger sandstones of attractive porosity and permeability. Production should present few problems and may well prove generally better than first estimates. But the more recent finds in deeper Jurassic and Triassic sandstones and limestone give rise to more uncertain problems of estimation, as at the Brae field. And these uncertainties may become greater as the search moves to smaller and more complex structures. At the same time, the question of determining how long a field may last and what percentage of reserves may be recovered is made more difficult in the North Sea, since companies plan offshore facilities to include equipment for re-injection of gas and water to maintain pressures early on. The opportunities for tertiary recovery methods to maintain production later on in the life of the field are thus more limited.

It is this need for pre-planning that presents North Sea development with its peculiar characteristics. Because of the water depths and sea conditions, production has to be planned from a single or a group of major platform structures containing in concentrated form

[1] All these fields are in awkward producing horizons where the production behaviour can be difficult to predict. The Argyll Field is a case in point. The production is from Zechstein Dolomite with some from Rotliegendes sandstone. Although highly productive in initial production tests, the field was, from the beginning, surrounded by uncertainty, and the group, the Hamilton Brothers consortium, decided on the use of a mobile rig. Early experience was reasonably optimistic. The group itself made a calculation of reserves of 32m. barrels with a life of about 7 years. Outside brokers put the reserve figures at twice this figure. Following the experiences of early 1977, the reserves were downgraded to around 20-25m. barrels and the production life may not last beyond 1978, unless additional oil is found in the area,

all the equipment for separation, water or gas injection and control associated with a field development. Because of the sea conditions, too, transportation should preferably be through a pipeline to avoid the period during which tanker loading may not be possible.

The development pattern places an extremely heavy capital investment burden on a project in the early years before production begins and cash starts flowing. Capital costs in the North Sea are as much as ten times the on-shore figure, or anything between $3,000 and $8,000 per daily barrel of production capacity compared to a few hundred dollars on-shore in the Middle East and perhaps $500 off-shore in the shallow waters of Nigeria or the Gulf.

On any discounted cash flow basis of calculation, returns for a given oil field are thus highly sensitive, first to any delays in achieving on-stream production, second, to any inflation in capital cost or a higher cost of borrowing and, third, to the number of platforms (the major item of expenditure) which may be required to produce the field. It is on all three counts that the first phase of development has been affected so badly during the period 1973-6.

As with the construction of nuclear power stations, the technical challenge has been less in developing entirely new technology to overcome the particular problems of North Sea production than the scaling-up of existing technology, developed in quite different conditions, to cope with the deeper water and worse weather conditions of Scottish waters.

Due in part to changes and refinement in design and in part to labour and productivity difficulties in on-shore construction, many early platforms were installed a year, and, in some cases, two years, behind schedule. The first two platforms for the Forties Field, scheduled for installation in the summer of 1973, were installed in the summer of the following year. The first Piper platform, due to be installed in June 1974, was delayed until the summer of 1975. The first platform for Brent, scheduled for July 1974, was installed during the summer of 1976, after the second platform had been ordered. It is regrettable that the platforms ordered from abroad were largely available on time. Those built in Britain were not.

Moreover, the problems of installation proved much more difficult than expected. Several major accidents occurred. One of the steel platforms planned for the Frigg gas field slipped to the seabed, several kilometres off target, because of a collapse in the floatation tanks, and could not be raised again. The articulated loading and mooring facility for the Beryl Field separated from its base and drifted, causing a six-month delay in commencement at the field. The laying of pipe in the early years fell far short of targets because of poor weather, the use of barges unsuitable for winter work and accidents which required the pipe to be raised again. Early problems were encountered in handling gas at the Ekofisk Field and in the use of the floating "spar" storage and loading system at Brent.

The delays, coupled with shortage of equipment and high rentals for such items as lay barges, appreciably intensified the sudden explosion in costs that hit many capital projects throughout the world in the 1973/74 period. Investment in the Forties Field, which had originally been estimated at £360m., rose to nearly £900m. by 1977.

The costs of Brent have virtually tripled from an initial estimate of around £500m. to well over £1,500m. The Dunlin and Thistle investment projections rose from around £160m. to nearer £500-£600m. each and the costs of the smaller Argyll and Auk Fields, initially thought to be around £15m., increased to nearer £50m. each.[2]

The result is that a feeling of considerable nervousness has been induced amongst the oil companies in trying to control costs and to resolve the unique and unexpected element in the timing of investment to the existing wide variations in cost caused by depth of water,

---

[2] See N. Trimble's *The Costs of North Sea Oil Developments, Past Trends and Future Prospects* (University of Aberdeen North Sea Study papers, no. 10, May 1976) and the study commissioned by the Department of Energy, *North Sea costs escalation study,* by Peat Marwick Mitchell and Co. and Atkins Planning, (Energy Paper Number 7, published July 1976). The Peat Marwick study is curiously coy about judging the relative weight of various factors and exploring their implications for future trends. It does make the interesting point that, in contrast to the oil industry's reputation for efficiency, much of the responsibility for the escalation can be attributed to the lack of good project management in companies and the tendency of management to pursue time considerations at the cost of estimating prices. Of the inflation of more than 140 per cent in projects in the 18-month period between 1973/5, about 30 per cent was estimated to have been caused by inflation in the unit price of materials, labour etc. The majority was caused by extra volume input of materials etc. due to initial underestimation of the difficulties and design changes. A similar point has been made in recent studies of cost escalation of the trans-Alaska pipeline system. The North Sea study nonetheless points out that the cost of repeat orders for similar steel platforms for the southern fields rose by a factor of 2·25 over the period of 1966-1973 almost entirely because of rises in input prices (at a time when inflation was less than half current rates). While it is hopeful that the rate of cost increases in the northern sector will lessen with repeat orders, this is unlikely to affect the general rate of cost increases in the country's manufactured goods.

distance from shore and field characteristics. Large differences between the Forties and the Ninian project costs emerged as their actual costs responded both to deeper water and the later time at which the projects were planned because of the high inflation rates.

With the quadrupling of oil prices, the coming on-stream of fields and more experience, there is now a stronger feeling of confidence about the returns and viability of existing projects. Construction times, in the U.K., where the early delays were longest, have tended to drop dramatically in respect of later platforms. The worldwide surplus of rigs, pipelaying barges and platform construction yards (particularly in the U.K., where they were expanded in anticipation of a continuing boom in demand which promptly collapsed) has resulted in considerably lower charter rates and tenders. Steel prices have fallen. Experience has improved design and the general explosion in capital costs of process plant has fallen as rates of inflation have moved down nearer to the level of general rates for manufactured goods.

Despite fears in the immediate aftermath of the 1973/4 crisis that oil prices might fall and the OPEC "cartel" break up, there seems little reason to believe that the present generation of fields under commercial development would be significantly endangered. Taking costs at their simplest basis of average capital costs (that is, dividing the total estimated recoverable reserves by total estimated investment) and average operating costs (which is more difficult to calculate, in view of the lack of experience and the rising curve over time as production declines after the peak is reached), the price of oil would have to collapse from the current $13-14 per barrel delivered to the U.K. to somewhere around half that rate before the major developments would theoretically have to be closed down as totally uneconomic. A large field developed early like the Forties Field, for example, has unit capital costs of a little less than $1 per barrel and average operating costs of about $1·30-1·50 on present estimates. At the more expensive end, a field like Ninian is unlikely to have total units costs of more than $4-4·50 per barrel (around two thirds of which would be capital costs).

These figures take no account of the company requirement of profit, financing costs and the relative impact of price falls as against the timing of investment. But even on the basis of internal rates of return on a discounted cash flow basis or by discounting future values back to a net present value under various assumptions of price changes, and assuming the present system of tax, existing developments seem relatively secure. Recent calculations made, most notably by Professor Colin Robinson and Dr. Jon Morgan of the University of Surrey, suggest that on a discounted cash flow basis, the returns of fields vary widely depending not just on unit costs but also the timing of the investment.[3]

Smaller fields, such as Auk and Argyll, with high unit costs but relatively low capital costs, early investment and a fairly short life tend to retain high rates of return, even if prices should fall rapidly towards the end of the decade. So, too to large or medium-sized fields such as Forties, Piper, Brent and Beryl—where capital investment has been largely completed—which stand to gain fairly rapid pay-backs within three to four years of production start-up and for whom a price fall after that would have to be drastic if it was to deter seriously the small amount of additional investment that might be required through the life of the field. The sensitivities of returns become much finer for the later fields, even for large ones such as Ninian and Statfjord,[4] and for smaller fields with high and relatively late capital expenditure such as Heather and Cormorant. For these, even a fairly moderate price decline could mean a substantial reduction in rates of return compared to a future in which oil price rises kept pace with inflation. But it would only be in the case of substantial price decline from 1977 through the next four or five years that the rates of return would fall to levels of 16 per cent or less which might be considered intolerable to the companies. By that time, most of the investment would have been made so

---

[3] "World Oil Prices and the Profitability of North Sea Oil", *Petroleum Review*, April 1976 and Professor Robinson's *The Economics of North Sea Oil and Gas*, a lecture given at the University of Cologne, 20th January 1976. Also Alexander G. Kemp's *The Taxation of North Sea Oil,* University of Aberdeen's North Sea studies no. 11, August 1976.

[4] Statfjord and Brent, the two largest oil fields in the North Sea, are also proving to be classic examples of the effects of continuous delays, costs escalation and,in the case of Statfjord, government intervention on field profitability. According to the latest estimates by Wood, Mackenzie in the first half of 1977, Brent oil production stands to achieve a d.c.f. return of 24 per cent and Statfjord of barely more than 20 per cent, compared to a d.c.f. return of over 40 per cent for the Forties Field and over 50 per cent for Piper. Amongst the smaller fields, the Heather Field, with low reserves, in deep water in the far north and still to be developed, stands to achieve a d.c.f. return of 23 per cent, while Auk, in shallower water to the south and already under development, stands to achieve a return of 38 per cent. The estimates are Wood, Mackenzie's own and may not agree with the operators'. Nevertheless they give some indication of the potential range of returns.

that the low incremental costs of sustaining production would still keep the companies producing.

The vulnerability of fields which have yet to be developed, and which are generally in the smaller to medium-sized category, is however much greater to changes in prices or escalations in cost. This partly helps to explain the continued degree of caution which companies tend to adopt towards new developments, despite the ending of much of the political uncertainty, the slowing down in the pace of inflation and the increased confidence in continued high world oil prices in the future.

Large fields such as the Forties, which can justify a pipeline on their own and which can produce as much as 400-500m. barrels of reserves from each platform, and fields like Piper and Beryl which are scheduled to produce as much as 800m. barrels of reserves through a single platform, continue to obtain a reasonable return of at least 20 per cent in all but the most drastic cases of a sharp and continuous fall in oil prices. Smaller fields of 2-300m. barrels of reserves, which may need two platforms to cover the field fully, or high cost fields in deep water without the benefit of a pipeline (and even larger fields such as Statfjord) could stand to see returns fall below 20 per cent if the price of oil fails to keep pace with inflation and could experience d.c.f. returns of less than 10 per cent if the price of oil fell in real terms by 20 per cent or more over the next ten years. A price rise does not give as much benefit as a price fall gives a disadvantage, unless it occurs soon after the field comes into production.

In these circumstances the future course of inflation as well as the future course of price rises becomes of paramount importance. Even if it is accepted that oil prices will undergo at worst a moderate fall in real terms and could rise to compensate for general world inflation over the next 10 years (a not unreasonable assumption at present), there must be a continuing concern about the U.K.'s rate of inflation and the ability of technical improvements to keep pace with the more difficult circumstances in which future finds may have to be developed.

The picture is not an easy one to read. Although charter rates on equipment have fallen and construction yards, running out of orders, are reported to be bidding at lower prices for new business, the high rates of U.K. inflation on manufactured goods and the fall in value of sterling has seen the cost of even existing fields rise by more than 15 per cent through 1976.

Tentative enquiries made by companies thinking of new projects suggest that the cost of the next round of development programmes could be substantially above the last, especially if the cost of major items, such as steel, starts to rise again as the world recovers from the recession of 1975/6 and U.K. wage inflation takes off again after the ending of Phase II restraint.

The development of new technology, particularly for sub-sea completions and tension-legged platforms which do not have depth limitations, could make a significant difference not only in bringing water deep fields into production but also in connecting smaller accumulations to the main facilities of existing fields, thus reducing costs. Already the development of large lay barges and supply boats and the construction of concrete platforms which do not require extensive installation work at sea has brought down the potential rise in costs (although not the absolute costs of developing North Sea fields). Development of the Argyll Field has shown the possibilities of developing small fields over a short time span using a mobile rig tied to wells. The Mobil group has already experimented with the use of sophisticated sub-sea completions.

As the pattern of field developments becomes more concentrated and as pipeline as well as platform capacity becomes available when the major fields pass their peak, there seems a strong possibility that the kind of small accumulations that have been found close to major finds such as Ninian, Brent and others could be tied in and that fields such as Maureen and Andrew in the case of the Forties pipeline or the Texaco finds around the Tartan fields in the case of the Piper line could be brought into existing transmission systems.

In mid-1977, it still looks unlikely that the drift of inflation will actually be reversed by new technology or that the use of sub-sea systems and tension that legs will bring significant reductions in total field costs however.

The technology for placing a degree of processing facilities on the sea-floor is still untried so that the next phase of development could go through the same learning curve problems which so bedevilled the first phase of North Sea oil development. The wells have to be drilled individually by a mobile rig. The facilities are expensive and maintenance, particularly that of parts replacement, requires special equipment and a delicacy of operation which may be just as vulnerable to North Sea conditions as pipelaying or platform module installation has been. The kind of cluster facilities being developed at present by Exxon may make it possible to produce small fields in deep water that otherwise could not stand the cost of full platforms. But they are costly and, at this time, it is doubtful whether they will make unit costs of development cheaper. Sub-sea development will come and, based on the experience of the introduction of concrete platforms in the current phase of development, they may well be accepted quite rapidly once they are seen to work. Yet the experience of the use of concrete platforms is equally that the take-off point tends to be later than initially hoped and the cost benefits are not nearly as great as expected.

Given these various factors of price, technology and cost, therefore, the build-up of North Sea production through the eighties may prove considerably less certain than present projections by economists might suggest.[5] As with exploration, the picture really divides itself into three phases—first, the fields already under development; second, the fields found but yet to be developed and third, the fields which may yet be discovered, particularly in the deeper water prospects west of the Shetlands or in the South-Western Approaches.

In the first phase, there are grounds for reasonable optimism. After initial delays had reduced first estimates of the build-up of North Sea production by around a third, experience is tending to suggest that the fields will be able to build up production rather faster than anticipated once they are in flow. There is still the possibility of delays in individual programmes—the construction of on shore facilities at Sullom Voe to handle production from most of the major East Shetlands finds is a particularly vulnerable spot and one which has already been subject to two years' delay.

Having started at a rate averaging barely 23,000 barrels per day in 1975 (production did not start until the second half of the year and only at low rates), in 1976 total U.K. output rose to an average 238,000 barrels per day. With the re-evaluation of Forties (whose peak output has now been upgraded to 500,000 from an expected 400,000) and Piper and the successful bringing on stream of the

[5] Professor Colin Robinson, for example, and Robert Belgrave, who is carrying out an analysis of future energy trends for BP, tend to assume a sharp rise in output in the mid-eighties as existing discoveries yet to be developed are brought in rapidly to push the total to over 3m. barrels per day and as new discoveries yet to be made begin their impact to take this total to as high as 4m. barrels per day—on the basis of no government depletion measures. The caution of companies developing fields, however, may express an instinctive depletion policy without government intervention—i.e. that their estimates of future price rises suggest that oil is better developed later rather than earlier. It is also highly unlikely that a sudden surge in development of recent discoveries will all take place at the same time, so that the peak may well be longer but lower.

Production Levels from Current U.K. Commercial Fields to 1985

(*thousand barrels per day*)

Field	1975	1976	1977	1978	1979	1980	1981	1982	1983	1984	1985
Argyll	10	22	30	29	27	24	22	20	—	—	—
Auk	—	26	40	40	15	13	—	—	—	—	—
Beryl	—	8	70	80	80	80	80	80	80	75	65
Brent	—	3	50	150	220	400	510	550	490	435	385
Claymore	—	—	40	90	115	140	120	110	90	80	70
Cormorant	—	—	—	—	20	40	60	60	50	45	40
Dunlin	—	—	—	—	60	80	120	150	150	150	135
Forties	13	175	450	500	500	450	422	372	327	288	253
Heather	—	—	—	25	50	50	50	50	43	36	31
Montrose	—	2	35	50	50	50	50	50	43	36	31
Murchison	—	—	—	—	—	16	64	80	96	86	78
Ninian	—	—	—	50	150	280	325	335	306	266	227
Piper	—	2	230	300	300	300	240	192	150	119	94
Statfjord	—	—	—	1	9	15	31	39	47	57	65
Thistle	—	—	—	110	180	200	200	160	130	110	90
Total (U.K.)	23	238	945	1,425	1,776	2,138	2,294	2,248	2,002	1,783	1,564

Source: Wood, Mackenzie and Co., June 1977

Beryl Field (after some initial disappointments on the first wells), output during 1977 is likely to reach 900,000 barrels per day, or the equivalent of half U.K.'s total oil consumption. Provided that Brent and the Shetlands pipeline system comes into action, that Ninian is brought on stream successfully and that Thistle achieves its ambitious targets of building up to 200,000 barrels per day within two years, during 1978 and 1979 output from existing fields should rise dramatically again to 1·3-1·5m. barrels per day in 1978 and 1·6-1·8m. barrels per day in 1979, climbing to a peak output (from existing discoveries) of 2-2·2m. barrels per day by 1981.

Due to the pace at which companies have planned the build-up of production, the peak rate of output is likely to last only three to four years for most fields, perhaps less in some like Thristle. The more rapid than expected peak of the Forties production and the later phasing of Brent will ensure that the plateau of all the fields is maintained through the turn of the decade at around 2m. barrels per day for about four years.

Both Forties and Piper, as well as Thistle, are expected to start declining at a rate of around 10 per cent per annum by 1980/1. Brent should pass its peak by 1983/4 so that, unless new fields are brought into production, the overall production from the 15 fields under development at present would go down after 1983/4 to around 1·5-1·6m. barrels per day in 1985, just as U.K. oil demand is likely to show a rise, and to 1m. barrels per day or less by 1990.

Because of the restriction of facilities on rigs and since gas or water injection into the wells is planned as part of the development from thes tart, the opportunities of sustaining the peaks are limited and tertiary recovery methods seem unlikely at present. There is however, on the basis of the history of other oil basins, a reasonable chance that the level of decline may prove more gradual than this and that the life of the fields (at present planned mostly for 15 to 20 years) may be considerably longer than first estimated. Satellite structures, such as have already been found around many of the major fields, could also be brought in either to buttress production during the early years of decline or to boost it towards the end.[6]

[6] Company policies towards the rate of depletion of fields, and the suspicion that they take the lowest-priced and most financially advantageous systems available, have induced Professor Odell to argue that fields are being produced, and platforms situated, in a way that will leave considerable quantities of

(*Continued on page 80.*)

Nevertheless, bringing on stream the additional discoveries still awaiting development or still to be found will be necessary to sustain production through the eighties and into the 1990s. Whether these are used to boost the mid-eighties peak to the 3m. barrels per day or more that some foresee (giving a substantial margin for exports) or whether they are used to maintain a rather low peak right through the decade is not only a question of Government conservation policy but also of the economics of production as determined by oil prices, technical advances and cost inflation.

Most long-term projections of oil output assume a given addition to reserves (around 5bn. barrels already discovered over and above fields committed to production with perhaps 5-10bn. still to be discovered), accept a lead-time between discovery and production start-up of perhaps 5 years and then deduce that 1m. barrels per day or more would be added to total output in the early to mid-eighties, largely to raise the peak.

On a reasonable assessment that a steady growth in new development programme announcements is now proceeding after the 1975/6 pause and that around 4-6 platforms will be ordered each year, each producing perhaps 70-100,000 barrels per day at peak, this may be true. But there is still some room for caution. Of the three dozen additional finds which have yet to have production, programmes announced or platforms ordered, only eight to twelve could presently be assessed as having a firm chance of being commercially developed early on (Alwyn, Andrew, Brae, Beatrice,

---

(*Continued from page 79.*)

potentially recoverable oil in the ground (Peter Odell and Kenneth E. Rosing's *Optimal Development of the North Sea's Oil Fields,* Kogan Page, 1976). His argument, as applied to individual fields such as Forties, has been vigorously attacked on technical grounds. But the general point that the calculation of recoverable reserves and the systems used for producing it is finally a question of economics must be a valid one (e.g. the cautious change in Ninian plans from a two to a three-platform investment). The question is how far financial considerations may mean oil being lost forever and how far companies take account of improved recovery in their original estimates and plans. On the former question, there is no evidence that oil will be lost forever because of the investment policies now being pursued. Indeed, the development of sub-sea well technology should mean that odd pockets of oil around fields will be brought in later. On the question of under-estimation of field reserves, a number of companies would argue that they take into account from early on a sizeable reserve figure based on expectations of improved recovery during the life of the field. Nevertheless on the basis of experience in other countries, the productive life of fields (which is in itself a financial issue of the point at which it is no longer worthwhile for a company to put in new investment and sustain high unit operaing costs) could prove generally greater than now estimated.

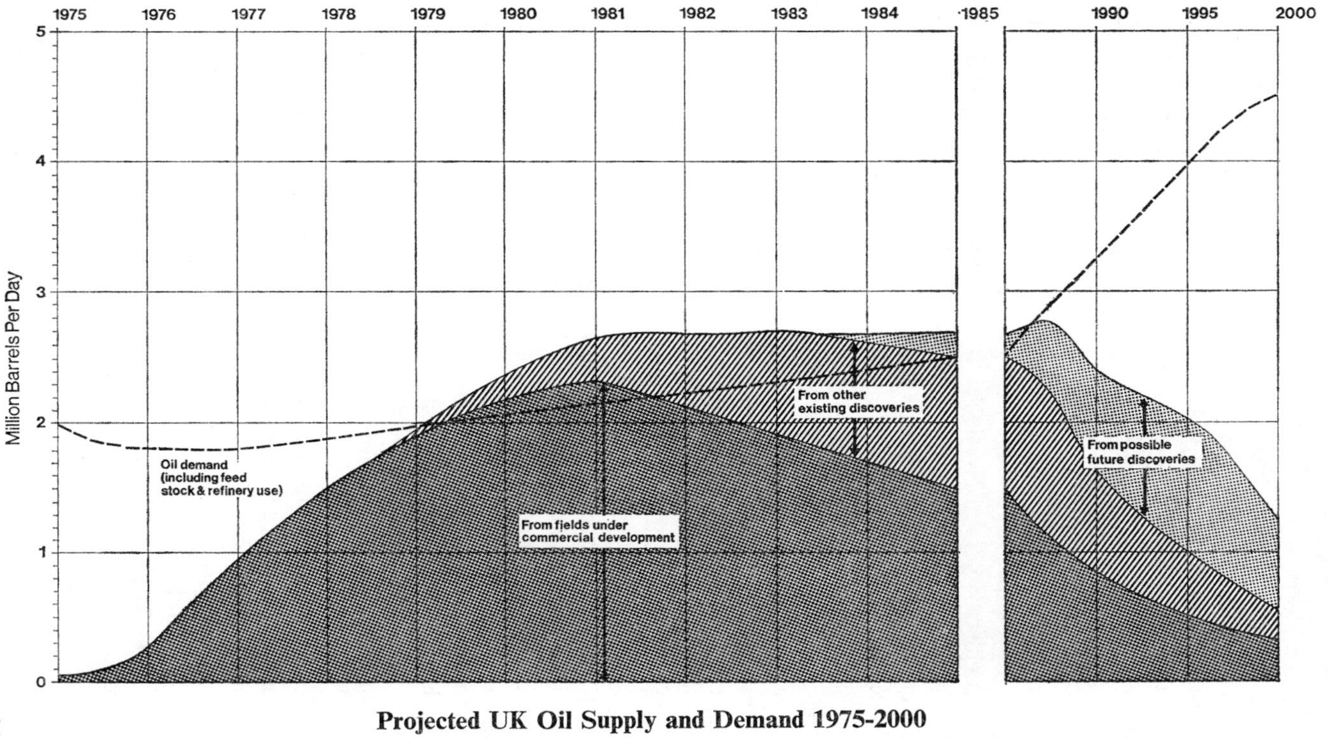

Projected UK Oil Supply and Demand 1975-2000

Buchan, North Cormorant, Hutton, Magnus, Maureen, Tartan, Tern, Fulmar and Thelma). Of these only one, Magnus, looks to be a major find in the 4-500m. barrels of reserve class with Alwyn, Tern, North Cormorant, Fulmar, Beatrice, Tartan, Thelma and possibly Brae, looking reasonably likely to have production plans announced over 1977-9. Many, if not most, may not come into production until the period 1982-6.

This is not to say that other recent finds will not prove commercially viable or that other substantial finds will not be made and planned for speedy development within the next two years. One of the peculiar factors in North Sea economics is that small fields, as Argyll and Auk have shown (and Buchan may yet show), can be developed quite quickly with a limited life of five or seven years, while larger fields can take much longer to appraise and develop.

Since the oil companies appear genuinely to be taking much longer to delineate their reserves and fields (partly because of the more complex geological nature of the finds); since the next few years may be a time of relatively soft oil prices and relatively high rates of U.K. inflation; and since the Government may take a more conservationist view in its attitude towards new development, the pick up in new platform orders could still be very gradual and the impact of output from new fields spread more evenly through the next decade. Production could thus level out at 2·5-3m. barrels per day rather than 4m. barrels per day in the early to mid-eighties keeping up this output to the early nineties. This might be welcomed by the Department of Energy (whose recent statements suggest that it is taking this projection more and more seriously), but it would also make a marked impact on the balance of payments and economic impact of North Sea oil and would have some serious implication for the platform construction and supply industry within Britain.

Even with this more moderate projection, too, there would still be an overriding need for new discoveries to ensure a surplus to internal requirements throughout the 1980s and an even stronger need for production from new basins to ensure a reasonable North Sea output into the 1990s.

Although the Government, at the peak of its fervour in 1974/5, was clearly thinking in terms of active intervention to control oil flows and iron out potential output peaks, more recent experience suggests that the slower momentum of development programmes is producing a conservationist result and that the companies are in no mood to rush a new generation of developments at this time. Given the uncertainties of predicting demand, reserves and production experience, the case for intervention would not appear strong, whilst the experience of past state controls, both in the U.S. as in this country, would not suggest that the Government's ability to make the right assumptions about future results is any better than the market's and, in the event, usually proves a great deal less flexible.

5 The Energy Context

In the development of the North Sea, it will be the international perspectives of energy supply and demand that will, more than anything, determine the price incentive for developing the oil and the ultimate value to a country like Britain in having major energy resources of its own. Ironically, the impact of the build-up of North Sea oil and gas from all sectors of the North Sea may well help determine this world picture of oil prices and supplies, certainly over the short-term and possibly over the longer term as well.

The area of energy projections, long or short-term, has proved a veritable minefield in which few have trod with their reputations unscathed. When North Sea exploration first got underway in the second half of the 1960s and when the first sniff of oil was smelt at the end of that decade, the opinion was that oil demand would go on growing at exponential rates and that its price would continue to be ruled by the low costs of almost limitless Middle East production. The Government's 1967 Fuel White Paper, hammered out after a meeting of energy chiefs at Selsdon Park, was in many ways a courageous and considered attempt to sort out trends and possibilities, particularly in so far as North Sea gas production was concerned. Had it been treated as a possible scenario rather than a firm projection, it might have gone down as one of the more notable attempts by Government to improve discussion and policy-making in industrial fields.

Had its forecast proved correct, too, the strategic and balance of payments value of Britain's oil and gas would have remained considerable but the commercial value of the high-cost new resource would have been much less and the country would have been grateful for the Fuel Ministry's efforts to ensure speedy exploration and exploitation regardless of economic rent.

As it was, the paper's central premise that the growth in oil demand could not be curbed and that oil would consistently undercut its competitors (a premise which was, it should be said, shared by almost everyone in the energy business at the time) was badly disturbed, first, during the OPEC price push of 1970/1 and then, far more dramatically, by the oil crisis of 1973/4. The effect was to give officials a lasting wariness of public projections (a similar reaction can be seen in the Treasury after the consistent failures of its national income forecasting in the last decade).

Yet that, in turn, has done nothing to improve the quality of forecasting since. In the immediate aftermath of the crisis, economists were once more worried by an oil price fall and the Treasury in particular began to express fears that the long-term trend in energy prices might again be downwards. As these fears have since subsided in the wake of renewed growth in demand in the industrialised West and further price rises by OPEC, so the consensus of opinion has now begun to swing back to the view that a long-term crisis of supplies is on the horizon, at least in the nineties and, quite possibly, earlier. The Department of Energy is once more emerging with long-term forecasts of its own and its mood is turning to one of conservation of its new oil and gas resources to see it through the longer term. Oil is in relatively easy supply at the moment, goes the argument, but by the end of the next decade the world will be facing the same gloomy prospect of shortage that it was previously facing for the end of the 1970s, only a decade later.[1]

It might be reasonable to assume that oil prices would at least keep pace with inflation and might move ahead of inflation as the day of reckoning comes nearer. If so, there is an obvious case for conserving supplies rather than developing an intermediate surplus for export which might leave the country well short of supplies when it most needs them later on.

The argument is neat and persuasive. But then so was the argument of the 1967 White Paper. Like that Paper it tends to assume that prices and supply/demand relationships move along an even line or curve, whereas the history of the last few years would tend to suggest that the movements take place in exaggerated rises

---

[1] The latest Department of Energy thinking is contained in a long policy review paper prepared for the meeting of the National Economic Development Council in March 1977. Wider long-term energy forecasts, all predicting trouble within the eighties to early nineties, include Robert Belgrave of BP in a detailed presentation of BP's forecasts for the U.K. and Europe to the Royal Institute on March 9th, 1977; the report of the workshop on alternative energy strategies *"Energy, Global Prospects 1985-2000"* (McGraw Hill, 1977); the OECD's *World Energy Outlook* (Paris, 1977) and a number of studies by the CIA, the Federal Energy Agency, Exxon, the Congressional Research Service and others in the U.S.

and falls as unexpected events (such as the cutting off of the Tapline pipe from Saudi Arabia and the Libyan cut-backs of 1969, or political upheaval) act on the margin of supply or demand and as producers and consumers respond in anticipation of what appears to be the medium-term trend. As with the 1967 paper, there is a natural tendency to ignore the fact that projections, by their nature, are warnings of what will happen if existing trends continue unabated and are not a prediction of what will actually come to pass. Where there is consensus of projections, the onlooker should beware, if only because the mere fact that there is consensus tends to bring about a positive response from the participants acting along similar assumptions.

Energy projections are particularly uncertain at this time because, in the aftermath of the 1973/4 crisis and during the prolonged recession in world economic activity which followed it, the basic factors of demand growth, new supply sources and Government intervention on such issues as price and conservation have yet to be clarified.

On the one hand, the recession has fundamentally altered the pace at which energy demand, and especially that of oil, is now expected to rise over the next two decades not only by providing a two to three year pause in growth due to the economic recession but also by shaving down the previous growth trend in energy. Pre-crisis estimates had suggested that energy demand in the non-communist world might grow to nearly 150m. barrels a day of oil equivalent for all primary fuels in 1985, and that the demand from Western Europe, Japan and the U.S. for imported oil might total 54m. barrels per day by then (18m. barrels per day in the U.S., 24m. barrels per day in Europe and 12m. barrels per day in Japan). More recent estimates have suggested that this point may not be reached until the 1990s, and that the oil import requirements of these areas in 1985 might be limited to around 10·5-11m. barrels per day for the U.S., around 11-12m. for Western Europe and about 7m. for Japan.

Over the short to medium-term, at least, many countries are now expecting a much slower rate of electricity growth, which in turn means a lower relationship between g.d.p. growth and primary energy demand. The economies of the major industrialised world are not predicted to grow at anywhere near the rate that was once foreseen early in the 1970s. The impact of new supplies of international oil from Mexico and the North Sea are thus likely to make a much stronger impact in curbing the growth in demand for OPEC oil than was once thought. Where pre-crisis predictions, for example, suggested that Western European primary energy demand might grow from around 25m. barrels of oil equivalent per day to nearer 60m. by 1990, primary demand fell to below 22m. barrels per day of oil equivalent in 1975 and is now thought unlikely to exceed 40m. by 1990.

In the U.K., the sudden pause in the rise in energy consumption has been even sharper, partly because of the more prolonged recession and partly because the combination of increasing natural gas use and lower electricity demand with some savings in end—use has had a relatively sharper impact on primary energy demand than elsewhere. Against a peak of around 4·9m. barrels of oil per day equivalent, primary energy demand in 1975 (including non-energy uses for oil and gas—largely in petrochemical manufacture) had fallen back to around 4·5m. barrels and is not expected to reach its 1973 peak again until 1979/80. From then on, depending on whether one assumes an economic growth rate nearer 2 or nearer 3 per cent and depending on how one sees electricity consumption growing, demand should not rise above 5m. barrels per day of oil equivalent until 1985 and could still be around 6m. barrels per day by the end of that decade.

On the other hand, nothing that has happened in the last three years since the oil crisis suggests that the major consumers have been able, or willing, to do much either about conservation in use or the more rapid development of alternative energy sources to oil, or that, over the longer term, they have lessened their dependence on oil imports to supply their needs. Nuclear power, although now planned to quadruple in capacity in both Western Europe and the U.S. by the mid-eighties, is still very small in its impact (less than half a million barrels per day of oil equivalent in Western Europe and less than 1m. in the U.S. in 1976) and is everywhere under environmental and political restraints, as the recent experiences of the U.S. and Germany have shown. Real conservation in end-use has not been extensive, and indeed in the U.S. there are signs that the few gains of the post-crisis period are being lost as the consumer returns to large car preferences. Above all, the dramatic decline in U.S. production of gas and the decline of output of indigenous North American oil has tended to subsume the fall in West Europe's import requirements as U.S. imports have risen by more than 1m. barrels per day each year.

As long as the U.S. continues to come into the market in a major way, and countries like Japan and Germany continue to supply their incremental needs from oil imports, the pivotal position of the Middle East and African producers of OPEC must obtain as will their ability to resist price falls due to lessening demand.

Despite a tendency amongst economists to regard OPEC as a cartel whose collapse would bring forth an imminent fall in prices, OPEC's members have never been able to agree amongst themselves sufficiently to adjust supplies to ensure that surpluses will not occur. It has been sufficiently unified to prevent individual members from openly pulling down the price. It is this unity (coupled with the fact that the adjustment of supply to demand was in any case carried out largely for them by their traditional concessionaires, the major international oil companies,) which partly explains their ability to prevent the price fall that was seen in other raw materials such as metals during the height of the world recession.

What remains true is that, as the producers have taken more and more control of oil, and as the marginal pressures of demand on supply have eased, the fundamental differences in attitudes and long-term self-interest of the OPEC countries have become more apparent. When, before, during the sixties and early seventies, it was in the interests of all producers to combine forces against the oil companies on questions of tax rates, expending of royalties, and prices, there is now much less unity of purpose. Countries such as Iran, with a large population and limited reserves for output expansion and with the potential to diversify away from oil, are now much nearer in attitude to similar countries like Algeria and Venezuela than they are to countries such as Saudi Arabia, with large reserves but limited prospects for economic diversification without internal social upheaval (through the use of large immigrant labour for example) or Abu Dhabi, with smaller reserves but limited use for excess revenues.

To the extent that internal needs for foreign revenue may be limited in a number of countries, so oil has become more and more of a political question. Saudi Arabia, for the moment, sees in a close relationship with the Western consumer its most important goal of limiting the spread of communism through the major Middle East countries like Egypt and Syria and a means—the only real means—of gaining ground in the Arab/Israeli conflict. Iraq has used oil to develop its special relationship with Russia and a more important role in the Gulf. Kuwait has consistently used oil to develop allies through straight subsidies and thus to protect its precarious strategic position in the Gulf.

For the moment, in a market of limited growth, these differences in self-interest have worked in favour of more stable prices as Saudi Arabia has acted to restrain oil price increases for political reasons, and because of its sensitivity to economic weakness in the West (which may be increased by oil prices) and its determination to prevent Iran from gaining leadership in the Gulf area—as was shown in its decision to introduce a lower price rise for its oil than most of its colleagues in the December 1976 OPEC meeting and its refusal to agree to any further increase in December 1977.

But what is also clear, and what was seen in the Stockholm meeting of OPEC in July 1977, is that the drop in demand for oil has not so far been sufficient to create conflicts between OPEC's members to lead to a significant erosion of oil prices. Even with the drop in average demand during the recession of 1974-6, the combination of unusual factors such as cold weather in the U.S., pre-emptive buying for stock in anticipation of a price rise, and a revival in economic activity was enough to push the demand on OPEC states to record heights during the latter part of 1976. Middle East output in the final quarter of the year topped 24m. barrels a day, only 15 per cent short of the region's theoretical producing capacity of 28m. and well above its previous average levels in the crisis year of 1973.

The December 1976 peak soon fell back as tanks were filled and conditions returned to nearer the underlying trends. Middle East production fell by no less than 5·5m. barrels per day (20 per cent) over a single month and countries like Iran and Kuwait, which had raised production to the maximum level feasible, suddenly found themselves experiencing falls of 1·5-2m. barrels a day of output each. The experience of the last quarter of 1976 is there as a reminder of the degree to which seasonal factors coupled with a combination of unusual circumstances can suddenly strain OPEC's resources.

In this situation the price and supply trends over the next 15 to 20 years could well be much more volatile than the consumers may suspect. As the balancing element in world oil supplies, the Middle East may find the next two or three years until the end of the present decade quite painful. The sharp rise in North Sea production, building up from around 1·1-1·2m. barrels a day in 1977 to around 3-3·5m. barrels in 1980/1 from the Norwegian and U.K. sectors, coupled with the coming on stream of Alaskan production in the U.S., starting at around 1·2m. barrels in 1977/1978 and building up to perhaps 1·6-1·8m. barrels by 1980, will do much to satisfy the incremental demand of both Europe and the U.S. and deprive the Middle East of much of its growth potential.

Over the longer term, however, all the present indications point to a return early in the 1980s to growing demand on the OPEC producers and a growing inability of alternative sources, including the North Sea, Mexico and China, to alter radically dependence on OPEC. Predictions again abound. The view of some oil companies is that the Middle East should be able to satisfy the increment without much strain well into the 1980s. Other bodies such as the OECD and the CIA in its most recent assessment, think demand might push against the limits of what OPEC will be prepared to deliver (although not necessarily the physical limits of production) much earlier in the 1980s.

The long-term projections of trends would certainly seem to bear this out. According to estimates made at the beginning of 1977 by Robert Belgrave of BP, world oil import requirements, at an energy growth rate of 3 per cent per annum until 1985, dropping to 1·5 per cent thereafter, are expected to grow from 26m. barrels per day in 1975 to nearly 30m. in 1980, 32·5m. in 1985, 40m. in 1990 and 50m. by 1995. Even if some of this increased demand could be met by increased exports from China and Mexico, it would hit hard against OPEC's producing capacity by the end of the 1980s and require a very considerable increase from the Gulf states, particularly Saudi Arabia, to ensure that this growth was met during the 1980s, especially as OPEC's internal requirements are expected to grow to 5m. barrels per day by 1990.

With a West European energy growth rate of 3 per cent per annum and assuming a fairly high production of around 7m. barrels per day in the mid-eighties, oil imports, having fallen to 9m. barrels per day, would still rise again, as indigenous oil production fell from the late eighties and demand increased, to around double this figure at the end of the century and nearly 15m. by 1990. In the U.S., even including Alaska and new discoveries elsewhere, oil imports could rise from 6m. barrels a day in 1976 to 10m. in 1985 and 14m. by the year 2000.

Just as these scenarios depend largely on Saudi Arabia raising production to keep pace during the 1980s (itself a questionable proposition considering the internal strains of expansion), the oil import demand projections depend on the ability of the United

States to develop an effective energy policy and West Europe to develop conservation and nuclear power.[2]

The point at which the western world lurches from meeting its incremental demand from indigenous or "secure" sources to meeting them once again from imports, and the price reaction at this point, will be determined more than anything by the responses of these two countries and by the way in which they view the future. As prices and supplies could be thrown into confusion even in the relatively near future should Saudi Arabia decide not to meet incremental growth or should political events cause a short-term disruption in supplies from any one part of the Middle East, so prices and supplies could be eased if the U.S. even seemed to be taking a firm grip on its energy supplies and to be acting to raise coal production and nuclear power investment and to cut oil demand. Just as the crisis points of 1970/1 and 1973/4 were the products of marginal shortages, so the picture could be radically altered either way, in the future.

Certainly, long before a crisis of supply is reached, the main participants will have reacted either by increasing prices or by increasing supply. Instead of prices moving along a curve together with inflation (which appears to be the general assumption about oil when North Sea projections are made), a perfectly possible scenario—it might be the most likely one—is that prices could fall in real terms through the rest of the 1970s as the first impact of

---

[2] The relative positions of the U.S. and Saudi Arabia were particularly difficult to assess during the summer of 1977. President Carter, in the Spring of 1977, at last produced an energy policy aimed at substantially curbing the growth of imports in the early 1980s from 8m. barrels per day in 1976 to 6m. barrels a day in 1985 (instead of the previously predicted 12m. at that time). While allowing for higher prices for newly discovered oil and for some rise in prices for gas, however, it was geared more to conservation in oil use and increasing the coal burn than in bringing forward new hydrocarbon supplies. Its passage through the Senate, after a relatively easy ride in the House of Representatives, was far from assured without fundamental revisions. Its lack of radical incentives for increased production and development of "unconventional" sources of oil and energy, however was regarded as a serious drawback and most outside analyses suggest that it is unlikely to achieve more than a curbing of import growth to around 10m. barrels per day in 1985 for the U.S. On the other side of the equation, relations between Saudi Arabia and the U.S. on oil and political questions remained good. The softness in the crude oil market in the summer of 1977 had also encouraged a general agreement amongst the major oil producers at the Stockholm OPEC meeting to express a relaxed view on price rises over the short-term. The continuance of Saudi Arabian goodwill remained critically dependent on the course of Middle East peace moves. Should the market have swung back to the producers' favour, there seemed little reason to believe that Saudi Arabia could exercise more than a moderating influence on price rises.

North Sea and Alaskan production is felt. The consumer might then relax with the feeling that all was well for another decade. Demand would rise again. The major producers, taking advantage of a seasonal or short-term pressure, would respond by jumping prices up again by a sharp 50 per cent in a single blow. This would in turn accelerate North Sea (and other) developments, which would have their response in greater supplies in the late 1980s just as the price might again be falling as consuming countries without indigenous reserves invested heavily to preserve their position.

Within this worldwide shifting pattern, the U.K. could be said —indeed Ministers never tire of saying it—to be relatively fortunate. It stands to be one of the very few major industrialised countries in the world to be virtually self-sufficient in oil. Around 1980 enough oil should be flowing from the North Sea to give it the equivalent of its internal oil consumption, even if a proportion is exported and part of its demand is still fed by imports. Gas supplies have an element of imports because of the Frigg Field contract, some 60 per cent of which is Norwegian. But the proportion is relatively small, at around 15 per cent of gas supplies in the early eighties, while the share of natural gas in the market is increasing once more Britain's coal industry, despite nearly two decades of rapid contraction, remains the largest in Western Europe with very considerable additional reserves discovered recently. The nuclear power sector, although riddled with problems of delay and safety and still making a relatively small contribution, at least has a history of success in its early stages (with the Magnox stations) and is expected to expand now that the second generation AGR stations are coming on stream. In addition, there is a small but useful contribution from hydro-electricity.

With this potential wealth of resources, the Government has, for the first time, been able to talk of the real flexibility of a four-fuel economy. It has, in theory at least, the opportunity of substantial exports during the mid-eighties, at around 0·5-1m. barrels per day, and hence the opportunity to conserve reserves for the longer-term by restricting those exports. Oil production, although short-lived in the sense of declining through the late eighties or nineties, should give it the time to re-establish a more viable coal industry and to develop safer and more advanced systems of nuclear power.

Whether North Sea oil and gas will provide this flexibility or whether the Government will use the time provided wisely is another question. Long term projection of energy supply and demand into

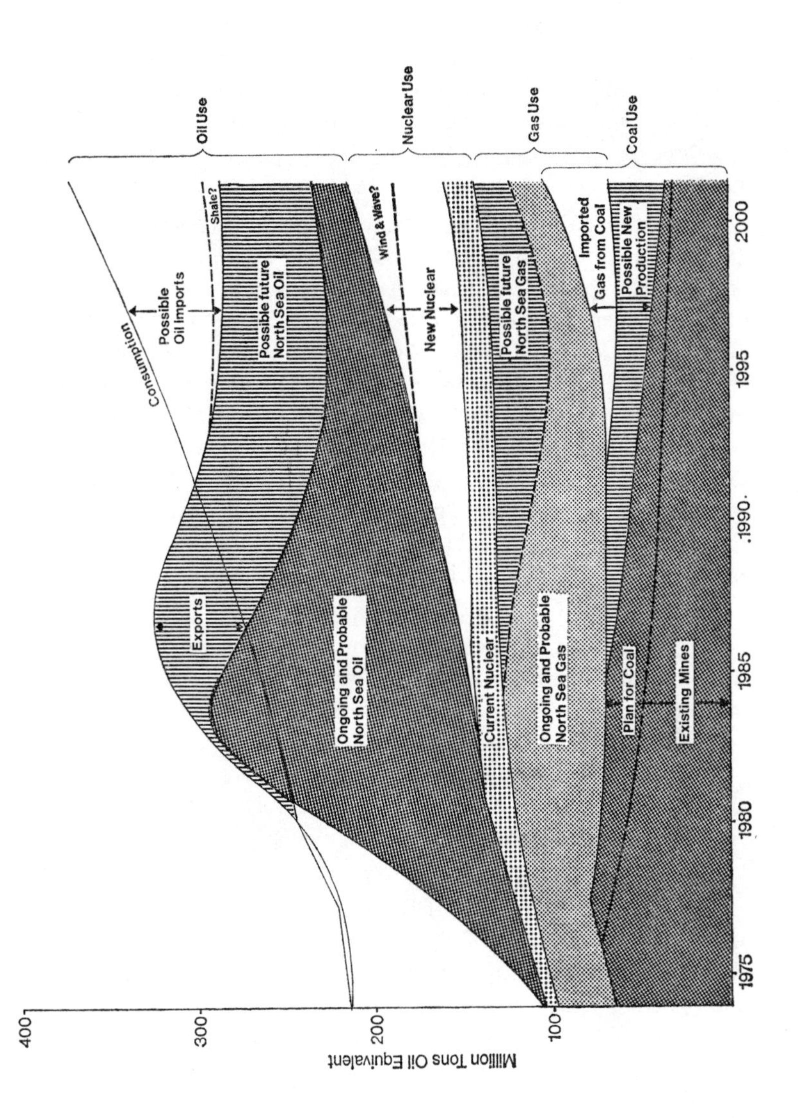

UK Primary Energy Uses and Sources at 2% Energy Growth from 1980

Source: British Petroleum, Talk by Robert Belgrave at R.I.I.A., March 1977.

the year 2000 are not of much value as predictions but they do at least give an indication of orders of magnitude if demand is not changed by technological developments and if supplies are not radically improved with discovery of major new oil basins (which could occur in deeper water) or through more rapid development of safer fast breeder reactors or nuclear fusion (which would give the consumer a renewable energy source).

On current thinking, these unchanged circumstances would leave the U.K., like the rest of the industrialised world, relatively well off through the eighties and heading into trouble in the 1990s. On the basis of an energy growth rate broadly similar to the averages through the 1950s and 1960s at 1·7 per cent per annum, Government projections suggest a rise in primary energy demand from 4.45m. barrels a day oil equivalent in 1975 towards 5m. by 1980 (barely more than the peak year 1973) and rising to between 4·9m. and 5·8m. barrels a day oil equivalent in 1985, between 5·5m. and 6·8m. in 1990 and between 6·5m. and 8·5m. in the year 2000. Estimates by BP and other companies would broadly support this, taking a middle line to 7m. barrels per day in 2000.

Even on fairly optimistic assumptions about new discoveries, the North Sea on its own could not keep pace with this demand growth beyond the early nineties unless there was a dramatic rise in coal output and nuclear capacity. Production on current assumptions (including new discoveries) would decline quite rapidly to around 1m. barrels per day by the end of the century and even if natural gas and coal manage to keep up supply levels, there would still be a gap of around 2m. barrels of oil equivalent per day which would have to be met by imports.

This depressing prospect of Britain returning to the international market just as the rest of the world is running out of supplies could be alleviated by a more rapid development of nuclear power, changes in demand patterns, or the discovery of major new oil provinces off North-West Europe. It could equally prove not to be a depressing prospect at all if worldwide supplies are plentifully available.

The more immediate question is really to what extent the North Sea will be called upon to meet demand during the next ten to fifteen years. And here the picture may be less comfortable than has sometimes been painted on present trends. Despite the presence of substantial energy sources other than oil in nuclear power and coal, it seems likely that oil will remain the balancing fuel of the British economy for some time to come. The National Coal Board, given new life by the oil crisis, has produced plans for stabilising output at about 135m. tons to 1985 (approximately 1·7m. barrels of oil equivalent per day). But this is critically dependent upon producing some 42m. tons of coal from new investments including new pits. Added to this it will require a further investment of around £400m. a year at 1976 prices to take it beyond this to an ambitious target of 165m. tons of coal a year at the end of the century.

The cost of the plan to achieve the 1985 coal target has already gone up by 50 per cent to £1·5bn. (at 1976 prices). Productivity in the industry has not improved as much as had been hoped and output of deep-mined coal has in fact declined to an expected 107m. tons in 1976/7 from nearly 120m. tons two years previously. The new production programme has been delayed, so that only half the 20m. tons of new pit capacity projected for 1985 will be operational then (although the Coal Board hopes to slow down the rate of exhaustion of existing pits to compensate).

The industry faces a short-term problem of surplus stocks and lower than estimated demand from its major customer, the Electricity Generating Authorities. In the long term it faces a problem of recruitment in view of its relatively high age profile. In addition, it continues to struggle with its ever present problem of high-cost, low productivity pits in Scotland and Wales—both areas of high unemployment requiring a diversion of resources to sustain jobs. Although the Coal Board remains confident that it is and will continue to be competitive, particularly following new investment, its recruitment difficulties in particular do not augur well for restraining costs while its wage-sensitive prices are becoming dangerously high.

Nuclear power, meanwhile, remains highly restricted in its potential contribution to energy in the eighties because of the lead times involved in building plant. Even though the electricity industry's second-generation AGR stations are beginning to come in with reasonable operating experience, the delays on the third generation (which may simply be an extension of the second) mean that its contribution to primary energy requirements in 1985 will be no more than around 300,000 barrels per day of oil equivalent while the most that could be expected in the following five years would be the addition of 100,000 barrels per day of oil equivalent.

Natural gas, on the other hand, could be expanded by the

Range of U.K. Energy Demand and Supply, 1975-2000
(*million barrels per day*)

	1975	1980	1985	1990	1995	2000
Demand:						
Energy uses	3·78	3·84–4·2	4·08–4·8	4·44–5·58	4·68–6·3	5·28–6·96
non-energy uses	0·32	0·42–0·48	0·48–0·6	0·6 –0·72	0·66–0·78	0·72–0·84
Total demand[1]	4·10	4·26–4·68	4·56–5·4	5·04–6·4	5·34–7·08	6·0 –7·9
Indigenous supply:						
coal	1·524	1·44–1·56	1·5 –1·62	1·38–1·74	1·32–1·86	1·2 –1·98
natural gas	0·636	0·72–0·78	0·72–1·02	0·72–1·02	0·66–1·02	0·48–0·9
nuclear	0·132	0·24	0·3	0·36	0·3 –0·54	0·3 –1·2
oil	0·024	1·92–2·28	1·98–3·0	1·98–3·0	1·2 –3·0	0·6 –1·8
Total indigenous production[2]	2·32	4·32–4·86	4·5 –9·4	4·44–6·12	3·48–6·42	2·58–5·88
Net imports (+) exports (–)	+1·8	+0·36/–0·6	+0·9/–1·38	+1·86/–1·08	+3·6 /–1·08	+5·22/–0·12

Ranges of energy demand are based on an economic growth rate of 2-3 per cent annually, energy prices remaining either constant or doubling in real terms by the end of the century and various fuel mixes

Ranges of supply are based on varying assumptions about reserves and technical potential. Figures for renewable resources such as solar energy are not included because of the uncertainties.

Source: Department of Energy paper to NEDC, 1977

addition of new supplies of associated gas through major trunklines, although this would be highly expensive. It is not clear whether the Gas Corporation wishes to accelerate the project to bear fruit in the early 1980s, preferring to stabilise supplies and to bring in additions as the older fields decline.

As long as the growth in the demand for energy remains moderate, the call on oil should be relatively manageable. Assuming that non-oil fuels contribute the equivalent of 2·6-2·8m. barrels per day (that is, assuming there are continuing problems with coal and a stabilising of gas supplies from 1981), and that the economy grows by no more than 2 per cent per annum over the next ten years, then the oil requirement in 1980 would be 1·8m. to 1·9m. barrels per day (around 200,000 barrels per day less than U.K. North Sea output at the time) and around 2·4m. barrels per day in 1985. This would be rather more than fields currently under development could supply. A rather larger quantity of crude oil might also be required if refineries were to produce enough petrol and naphtha (where the growth is highest at present and there are no real substitutes) to meet internal demand. With the addition of medium and larger-sized fields already discovered, such as Magnus and Tern, indigenous oil supplies should be enough to cover this.

If a rather higher economic growth rate of around 3 per cent is sustained, partly because of the benefits of North Sea oil, the position could be much tighter without a fairly forceful development of additional discoveries. Should other fuels be constricted, oil would be called on to meet demand of over 2m. barrels per day in 1980 and over 3m. barrels per day in 1985. On the estimates of ultimate reserve potential, this is feasible, but would require the addition of 1·5-2m. barrels per day above that which can be expected from fields under current development. Even with a reasonable expectation from fields found but not yet committed to production, demand might still require a further 0·5m. barrels per day of production from fields yet to be discovered.

Such a picture suggests a number of interesting implications. One is that, from a pure energy point of view, the country cannot afford to relax entirely its efforts on coal and nuclear power and this may necessitate a fairly high price for oil. The Coal Board and the nuclear industry at the moment could claim considerably lower production costs than oil. In power stations, for example, the latest figures for average generation costs of existing CEGB stations were put at

0·67p per kilowatt hour for nuclear, 0·97p per kilowatt hour for coal-fired and 1·09p for oil-fired stations. The figures relate to historic capital charges rather than future costs and in the light of the coal industry's need both to recruit labour and to fund a massive investment programme and the experience of nuclear power station construction of late, there would seem little room to pass on the benefits of North Sea oil to the customer in the form of lower energy prices without endangering alternative investments in other fuel sources.

Secondly, in the area of energy growth possibilities, there may be much less margin of flexibility than some commentators and politicians have suggested, following the North Sea discoveries. At low growth rates and continuing expansion of alternatives, there could be room for sizeable net exports of perhaps 10 or 20 per cent of North Sea oil output. At higher, though not outrageous, growth rates and a levelling off in non-oil supplies, the North Sea may have considerable difficulties in filling the gap unless the second-generation field developments are accelerated and new exploration is encouraged.

This, in turn, raises a doubt over the often raised issue of conservation and depletion controls.[3] The pause in second-generation development and the delays incurred in the first generation of production have already caused the Department of Energy to tone down some of its previous remarks on the need to hold back activity so that

[3] The issue of depletion controls has aroused surprisingly little debate in the U.K., partly because the Government itself has been indecisive and has presented its need for controls purely as a residual power should events require it to intervene. The issue is, however, opened up in Colin Robinson and Jon Morgan's *Economic Consequences of Controlling the Depletion of North Sea Oil and Gas* (Trade Policy Research Centre, Guest Paper no. 3, January 1976), which takes a largely free market view. Part of the problem in the discussion at present is the difficulty of determining whether there will be a realisable net surplus of production for export in the mid-eighties (a substantial proportion of oil—as much as 40 per cent—is likely to be exported in any event). The problem is partly in determining how oil companies at present are reacting in their North Sea investment decisions to their price projections and partly in the current fall in real terms of world oil prices. Robert Belgrave, in his address to the Royal Institute, suggested that the hump in oil production in the mid-eighties would certainly open up the depletion option. But he suggested that even on BP's figures showing a fairly sharp excess of production over consumption representing a potential surplus of around 11 per cent of reserves, cutting this back to the consumption levels would only prolong self-sufficiency by about two years and make the decline in oil production slightly less severe. For reasons cited in the last chapter, such a surplus may not occur. It should be added that depletion controls on fields already in production present technical problems.

oil output does not greatly exceed the projected internal demand, since it now believes that output may not exceed it to the expected degree.

The Government has taken extensive powers to control depletion both by delaying new investment approvals and by ordering a reduction of output within limits and through its indirect powers, recently put into practice, to limit gas flaring. Conservation has entered the canons of political clichés of our day (not least because of fears of Scottish resentment over the pace of development). In its latest energy projections, the Department makes basic assumptions about the long-term—that energy prices will rise by between 50-100 per cent in real terms by the end of the 1980s and that North Sea will leave the country returning to the import market in the 1990s—which imply a strong view that indigenous resources should be stretched out as far as possible to prolong their life.

Besides the highly speculative nature of some of these assumptions about the long-term trend in energy prices (if they were true, the Country might be considered better off not producing the North Sea at all for the moment), it is hard to see whether intervention on depletion should be aimed at speeding up development or slowing it down. It may be that the interest of oil companies in the pace of resource depletion is not a perfect indicator of long-term interests of the nation or the consumer. While the companies in the first generation development undoubtedly went for a rapid rate of build-up, it could just as well be argued (as Professor Odell, for example, has done) that their current interests are for slower development considering their worldwide surplus of supplies.

The most effective form of checking the interests of the international corporations must be to provide sufficient competition from companies, such as small independents, with different interests in developments as well as different views on geological prospects, nor is it clear that the interests of a government department are necessarily the same as the long-term interests of a nation. On the basis of past experience in price intervention in the nationalised industries and the distortions caused by interference in the Electricity Generating Authorities' choice of fuel, the opposite might be held to be the case. The Norwegian experience has shown that the presence

---

[4] The pattern of disguised interests in a country such as Britain where policy is decided by competing pressures behind the scenes is always difficult to determine. In the future course of depletion policy, however, the main pressures may well arise as much from the state of the coal industry (the relative state of stocks,

(*Continued on page 100.*)

of a state oil company can militate against government policy for reasons of the state company's corporate interests at the time.[4]

Even assuming that some form of depletion policy is desirable, it is difficult to see just how it should be expressed. Should gas supplies be boosted by a subsidised investment in a trunk line gathering system when the Gas Corporation may prefer to hold a steadier course? Should existing fields be cut back and new fields developed (which would go against the Government reassurance) or should new development be halted with the danger that exploration would slow down and flexibility be lost? How, in view of the lead times associated with new oil field development, would projections of future demand and supply be developed with some assurance of their accuracy?

It may be that future discoveries and developments in the North Sea give a much greater margin for error. It may be that the future course of North Sea development makes worries about the longer term either more intense, because of the failure to find new oil in deeper water basins or less intense, because of substantial new basin discoveries.

The real lesson of the energy projections now being produced may simply be that, despite the air of bonanza that has accompanied the period of major finds, the country still does not know enough about the size of its potential resources either to plan confidently over the long-term, or, to assure itself an easy situation over the medium-term. Despite the present rapid build-up of output

---

(*Continued from page 99.*)

the wage pressures from the miners and the attitude of the electricity authority to flexible fuel use), and the relative strength of Scottish nationalism, as from any view of the economic or energy needs for depletion controls on oil. To this BNOC will add its own corporate interests, which have yet to be made clear. In Norway, Statoil, requiring a stronger presence and more oil than it had early on, was urging a faster rate of licence allocation in its early years (1973-5) than the Norwegian Government wished. More recently it has come into conflict with the Industry Ministry both in its desire for virtual monopoly of exploration north of the 62nd Parallel (against the Government's desire to see some countervailing force and competition from the majors) and in its desire for piping gas and oil from Frigg and Statfjord to the mainland to promote refinery and petrochemical investment there (the Government is less willing partly because of the environmental risks, partly because of the poor market prospects and partly because of the delays in Statfjord's development that it implies). BNOC, because of its participation agreements and Burmah and NCB holdings, may have less interest in more oil for itself as such. Its ambitions to develop as a separate entity may well encourage it to seek new exploration licences in which it can have controlling interests and to urge production controls on existing fields to make room for its own growth.

and the sharp drop in demand growth, it still cannot be sure of the flexibility that is the key to a four-fuel economy. Until the limits to its new resource are more precisely determined, which may require improving the environment for investment, the Country's options must remain a lot less favourable than Government statements would have the consumer believe.

6 Policy Fandango

Major oil discoveries, like Eve's apple, rarely leave a pleasant taste to those who would eat of them. So long as oil is but a gleam in the country's eye, all is incentive and welcome for foreign investment and foreign know-how. Once oil is found, the cries change to resentment, greed, and divisiveness within the host country as the politicians quarrel over how the spoil is to be divided. The critics comment on the "give-away" nature of the original licence terms and officials decide that they need ever more restrictive powers to control the beasts they have let loose to pillage the country of its rightful wealth.

Why the oil companies, who have experienced the same pattern in almost every country in which they have ever operated, should have expected Europe, and especially the U.K., to have been different must be something of a mystery. But they did expect it to be different and acted on this assumption almost without exception. They proved to be mistaken.

Britain, of course, has proved to be the most obvious, or the most blatant, example of landowners seized with envy of their tenants when the untilled land they had rented proved to bear fruit beyond their first imaginings. The story of the last three years in the U.K. North Sea could largely be written in the light of the attempts of both officials and politicians trying to recover the ground they felt to have been lost for a derisory sum.[1]

---

[1] This is not to imply that the oil companies are the innocent victims of unscrupulous politicians. The history of Libya, Iran and elsewhere suggests the opposite—that companies are quite prepared to take maximum advantage of the room for tax avoidance and lack of controls available to them. The problem arises from a chicken-and-egg situation—in order to induce foreign investment, countries offer easy initial terms and then change them as the play progresses and this in turn encourages companies to seek as early a pay-back as possible to counteract the political risk. There is no reason to believe that companies would not have done the same in the U.K. Indeed, the statements by several

(*Continued on facing page.*)

In the event, virtually all the countries of North-West Europe (with the exception of newcomers such as Greenland) experienced the same process of an initial offer of licences on attractive terms followed by concentrated and at times painful efforts to change the rules once oil had been found. Ireland, Denmark, Germany, the Netherlands (at least on-shore), Norway and Britain all offered discretionary licences to begin with on attractive terms with no requirement for state participation and few if any special tax provisions.[2] No country has gone to quite the same lengths as Britain in changing the license terms and effecting participation in licences already granted. Some have been content to change the rules on new license issues as they have been awarded and to gain an additional economic rent through tax rather than equity shares in previous acreage awards. All countries have gone through a period of intense re-adjustment and political uncertainty in consequence of the North Sea discoveries.

Despite Norway's reputation as a hard-nosed and decisive negotiator of national interest with the oil companies, at least part of its actions have resulted from political uncertainty and changing pressures rather than considered policy. To compensate for the relatively easy terms on which the Ekofisk blocks were awarded, it used the issue of granting exports for the Ekofisk oil and gas in 1972 as the occasion for prolonged and shifting haggling with the

---

on the tax question indicate that some were basing their calculations on little if no tax. But it is important to remember that, even at this stage, no company has yet made a profit out of North Sea oil and that, at the time of the changes in policy, the question of profits and returns had been confused by the course of inflation, delays and uncertainties over the future price of oil.

[2] Royalty rates in the early rounds varied from a sliding scale of 0-16 per cent, depending on volume, in the case of the Netherlands; 5 per cent in the case of Denmark and West Germany; 10 per cent in the case of Norway; and 12·5 per cent in the case of the U.K. Tax rates varied from 48 per cent in the Netherlands; 50·6 per cent in Norway and 50 per cent in the U.K., although these were complicated by the varying depreciation provisions and local taxes. A study carried out by consultants for Shell at the time of the U.K. fourth round indicated that the U.K. terms were broadly the same as the Norwegian and rather tougher than other European countries. Most countries have now changed the terms, introducing compulsory state participation and a special tax. These include Norway (state participation from the 1969 round, higher royalties in 1972, and a special tax in 1974/5); the Netherlands (state participation from the start at 40 per cent, increased to 50 per cent in 1976); Ireland (state participation up to 50 per cent and a special oil tax, 1975); and Greenland (state profit share on oil production of 55 per cent, with progressive relinquishment over 10 years and state participation up to 50 per cent in the allocation awarded in 1975).

Phillips group to ensure a state share in the pipeline system and hence a potential control over prices and flows.

The discovery of major oil and gas reserves off Norway played a substantial part in the unexpected defeat of the Norwegian Government in the EEC referendum of 1971, just as that defeat, and the element of popular distaste for industrial development, in turn played a not insignificant part in the succeeding Norwegian Government's development of a conservationist approach to oil. The main impetus for this was unquestionably the Norwegian Finance Ministry's deep concern over the potential impact on inflation, wage rates and employment balances of an unrestricted development of oil fields and a massive inflow of foreign currency that this might bring. But the continual delays in offering new licences, the hesitations in actual awards (the last round saw only a quarter of the licences offered actually allocated) and the continuing debates about when and how to start drilling north of the 62nd parallel owe as much to lack of confidence by the Norwegian Government as to policy determination. The creation of an ambitious state oil company in Statoil has to some extent further intensified these internal conflicts in the Norwegian Government as differences have grown between the Ministry for Industry and Statoil over gas pipeline investment, landing points, downstream investment in refining and petrochemicals and the degree of monopoly that Statoil should enjoy north of the 62nd parallel.

In Holland, the discovery of the immense gas reserves on-shore at Groningen induced a retroactive attempt by the Government there to increase its stake through negotiated participation and this procedure has been extended to other on-shore fields. Off-shore, the Dutch Government originally decided, like the U.K., to award licences on a discretionary basis without state participation, but a change of Government in early 1965 and its decision to insist on state participation, in the Amended Continental Shelf Act led to two years of continuous argument and delay before the first licences were awarded in the summer of 1967.

In Ireland the reaction to the terms on which most of the off-shore was originally awarded to Marathon in 1965 led to considerable political argument when prospects were heightened by what was happening in the North Sea. As in the U.K., the control of gas purchase prices was used to limit the potential profits from the Kinsale Head gas find of Marathon's while the award of new licences in 1975 was itself preceded by a year of constant debate and argument over potential terms and reconsideration before the blocks were allocated.

In Germany and Denmark, where the entire Continental Shelf area was originally allocated to single consortia in each of the countries, worse problems were avoided only because so little was found.

The political tensions and the arguments over tax and licence terms would seem to be the inevitable product of the nature of oil exploration itself. Oil exploration, unlike other extractive industries, is based on the discovery of potentially sizeable reserves in traps of a very small area. Apart from the risks in finding oil, which depends partly how much is known about a basin and therefore at what period in its development licences are issued, there is the enormous difference in potential profitability between finding a major field, a medium-sized one or a small accumulation. This aspect is highlighted particularly in an area of the North Sea where to the risks of exploration are added the risks of development and the high capital costs, all of which make profits much more sensitive to the size and nature of the reservoir.

Oil is basically an international commodity, which means both its price and the relative enthusiasm of companies to explore in an area are dependent on world-wide circumstances. This, again, is highlighted by the differences in approach of international major oil companies, whose investment policy will be partly determined by their relative supply position at any one time and their marketing position in the host country (e.g. whether they will be forced to take the new supplies for their refineries if oil is found), and the smaller independent exploration companies, with quite different supply and financial needs.

Moreover there is the peculiar emotion which surrounds oil discoveries. Because oil production is a capital intensive industry with relatively low running costs once the oil comes on-stream and because it can flow in large quantities at a high price, there has always been an air of bonanza around a major find in which the cash flows seem to dwarf the capital expenditure. Because energy is the single most important resource in an industrialised society, there is an inevitable tension between an industry structured around international flows of oil and maximising the benefits of international diversity and a nation anxious to produce the resource according to its own needs. This aspect is again intensified by the geographical distribution of major reserves in which oil and gas have often been found in countries for which it remains their major source of wealth.

However much commentators may calculate the best economic framework for oil development or oil taxation, they will not be permitted to ignore the political factors surrounding oil production with their peculiar non-commercial aspects.

No one in these conditions has found a perfect system for licensing and taxation which can give the right encouragement to original exploration yet still ensure the right economic rent and control for the host country once oil is found. Auctioning licences, production sharing agreements, sliding royalties and carried state interest (the state being given the right to take a set share if commercial fields are discovered) have all been tried. But all have tended to be varied during the course of the licence as the international price of oil has changed, the host country has found more or less oil than it expected or the size and profitability of discoveries has proved larger than first thought.

The most effective way of ensuring the maximum economic rent from exploration—that is the margin between, on the one hand, what the company requires to search for the oil, produce it and retain a profit that allows for its risk as well as investment and on the other what it can obtain for its product in this market—may well be the auctioning system as practised in the U.S. and tried on a limited experimental scale in the U.K. in 1972. In this way a government can be fairly confident that it will establish the value of the development rights it is handing out. The general market prices will then be adjusted automatically as new licences are given at various stages of development, thus avoiding the need for government itself to build up the knowledge and take responsibility for the valuation decision. The bidding need not necessarily be in the form of cash—it can, for example, take the form of companies offering different percentages of royalties on any oil found or different rentals—and all sorts of conditions on performance guarantees, and the financial strength of the applicants can be built in. But to ensure the maximum efficiency, cash bidding open to a wide range of applicants is clearly the favoured way.[3]

---

[3] See Kenneth W. Dam's *Oil Resources—Who Gets What How?* (University of Chicago Press, 1976). Also a report by James B. Ramsay of Michigan State University for the American Petroleum Institute and M. Crommelin's "Offshore Oil and Gas Rights: A comparative study," *Natural Resources Journal*, October 1974. Bidding, at present, is in fact the exception rather than the rule in the world and outside the U.S., only Canada and the U.K. have used it, and then only experimentally. The reason seems more the political antagonism to selling the country's "birthright" than economic considerations.

The argument against auctions takes several forms. One, pushed most strongly by the major oil companies when advising governments before the first rounds of licences in the North Sea, is that the money bid is money that would otherwise go in exploration and that the exploration effort is commensurately reduced. This may be partially true for large companies which work on total exploration budgets and which, in an auction, tend to concentrate on fewer blocks. But, given international competition for an area, the experience of neither the U.S. nor, indeed, the 15 blocks auctioned in the U.K. North Sea is that successful bidders hold on to territory or are slow to develop. The opposite may be nearer the truth, at least on the expensive blocks, since companies are then anxious to confirm the value of their acquisition (as Shell-Esso were on the golden block for which they paid £21m. in the North Sea).

Another argument against auctions is that they tend to favour unduly the major companies with large resources at the expense of competition from smaller companies. But, again, on the basis of the U.K. experiment, this is not entirely true. Large companies tend to bid most on the most obviously attractive blocks. On the other hand the alternative discretionary system, with its emphasis on giving blocks to companies most capable of developing them and companies with refining and marketing assets in the host country, is even more prejudiced in this direction. The weight of the majors in any case reflects a natural weight in the field, whatever the licensing system (unless the market is deliberately distorted against them). The U.K. and U.S. auctions have shown that smaller companies are quite prepared to bid relatively large sums on the basis of their knowledge and instincts.

Still another argument is that, under an auctioning system, the government loses its control over the pace at which the blocks are drilled and the relative competence of the operators. But this can be overcome by imposing competence rules and drilling commitments on applicants. Nor is it necessarily a bad thing to have companies willing to undertake exploration even if they do not have the resources to develop fields themselves and then have to sell off a share in the discovery to someone who has. From the point of view of competition, a major oil company without need of additional oil is more likely to sit on its assets purchased through auction than a smaller investment group for whom there is more urgency in establishing its main aim—the upgrading in value of its asset through exploration.

The fundamental objection of governments to the auctioning systems lies rather on political, administrative and emotional grounds. Under a free bidding method, it is difficult to ensure a national representation in licence allocation, and this is particularly important for European governments such as the U.K. which have been anxious, on balance of payments as well as political grounds, to see as much local participation as possible.

At an early stage in the development of a basin, an auction would tend to raise relatively little money (even the experimental auction of 1972 showed the majority of blocks raising less than the cost of a single well),[4] so that the security from later political resentment that must be an essential aim of any licensing method, would not be achieved as any later discovery on these blocks would be greeted by even louder howls of the nation's birthright being sold for a song. This is particularly so in Europe where there is a strong public distaste for property development gains and for lotteries of basic "national assets". In the later stages, the sums raised would of course be larger, but by then the fact of oil having been discovered would make selling licences even less acceptable as the demand for more national participation would have risen. Nor do large sums raised necessarily abate the feeling that the resource has been underpriced. Had Shell-Esso found a major field on its golden block, the bid of £21m. would still have seemed small in comparison with the cash flow that a large field brings, although large by the standards of the time.

---

[4] The auction, which raised a total of £37m., was deliberately designed to cover a range of blocks with varying geological prospects. Extrapolation of its results for the whole round is difficult since a high proportion of the fourth round was in unknown western waters and since a number of companies took the view that their bidding practice would influence allocations of discretionary blocks. Of the 15 blocks auctioned, nine blocks fetched less than £1m., the average cost of a one-well commitment. Five fetched £51,000 or less. The lowest successful bid was £3,200, the highest was £21m. The disparity between bids for the blocks (the second highest bid for the £21m. block was £8m.) would tend to confirm the lack of geological knowledge at the time, although the industry did show general agreement in their bidding on which were the important blocks. On the basis that most of the blocks on offer were in the more attractive northern area (which received the highest bids), the 158 blocks finally licensed in the northern basin might have fetched around £250m. in total. Drilling since then has not suggested that companies have been slower to drill on their auction than their discretionary blocks—indeed the opposite may be the case. It is interesting to note, however, that of the 9bn. barrels of recoverable reserves currently being produced or planned for production, around half has been found on blocks awarded in the third round.

Added to this has been the desire by European officials to maintain a more discreet control of oil companies through a discretionary system which allowed them to use a system of favours in future licences based on behaviour in previous rounds.

For all these reasons, European governments, led partly by the British, initially adopted a discretionary system which sacrificed immediate economic rent for what was regarded as stronger control over national participation and oil company behaviour in exploration and development. Since the early rounds, this system has been progressively refined and more and more burdens placed on the companies in the form of state participation and licence obligations as development has proceeded. The degree of toughness in national terms has depended both on the success of exploration and their own view of their internal needs for rapid or slow development.

In the case of the Dutch, with the advantage of the massive Groningen Field already discovered on-shore and high initial exploration interest off-shore, state participation requirements were introduced from the first in an option for the state to buy in if a commercial gas field was found. Following Dutch tradition, only exploration licences were awarded with the right of the company to change these into production licences once a find was made—at which point higher rentals and the state participation option came in. The Dutch have also chosen, partly because of their more limited Continental Shelf area, to award acreage in smaller licence terms, although they have not (until the latest round when the stake participation has been raised to 50 per cent) much altered the terms with each new round, partly because exploration success has been gradual rather than spectacular.

The Norwegians, meanwhile, following the early discovery of the Ekofisk and neighbouring reserves and their worries about the impact of the finds on a small, high-employment country, have expressed their policy of "make haste slowly" largely through slower and much more limited licence awards.

Without the need to encourage new finds, and therefore requiring the offer of continuing high inducements or to create competition amongst the exploration companies, the Norwegians have also progressively tightened competition with varying degrees of state participation up to 60 per cent, and with the introduction during the last licence round of variable (although still relatively limited) royalty rates of between 8 and 16 per cent. They have, further, brought in new tax rules and tighter control and have developed a state oil company charged not only with exploration but also with creating downstream investment in petrochemicals and refining.

Inspired largely by the Norwegian example, Greenland—which shares many of Norway's worries about the impact of oil development on local society and has what is considered highly attractive acreage—has adopted many of the same provisions of state participation and controls, as have the Irish in their latest licence allocations.

The U.K., on the other hand, has come to this route late in the game and that only after it had issued some 90 per cent or more of its prospective acreage in the North Sea south of the 62nd Parallel and a sizeable proportion of its new basin areas in the Celtic Sea and west of the Shetlands. The fact that it did so, and on such apparently easy terms, has aroused endless debate and criticism, particularly following the Public Accounts Committee's report of 1972.

What is often forgotten in the general air of disillusionment with previous government policies which followed this report, is that, set against the primary aim of rapid and extensive exploration off-shore (an aim which went almost unchallenged at the time in political or official circles), British governments were remarkably effective and imaginative.

For countries like Norway—with a rare and welcome combination of high geological prospects (at least after Ekofisk was found) and limited internal needs for new employment, revenues and indigenous energy sources[5]—the extent of economic rent that can

---

[5] Norway, with a population of 4m. and with the largest and most prospective Continental Shelf in Europe, by the end of 1976 had drilled 160 wells resulting in 30 finds with proven reserves of 5·4bn. barrels of oil and 22·8 trillion cubic feet of gas. Oil reserves are currently equivalent to 160 years of the country's current oil consumption of 140,000 barrels per day. Despite considerable delays at Ekofisk and Statfjord, Norwegian oil production by the end of 1976 totalled 280,000 barrels per day, twice its consumption. By the early 1980s, production should equal five to seven times its consumption, which is equivalent to around a quarter to a third of its total exports and contributed more than 20 per cent of the Government's gross income. Already the oil sector accounts for the same proportion of gdp as agriculture, forestry and fisheries put together, although its share of employment is limited to 6 per cent. Current policy is to limit production of oil and gas together to an equivalent of 1·8m. barrels per day of oil and oil equivalent. More recently, however, the effect of the delays in production on a country suffering some of the effects of oil recession and lack of demand for platforms and oil equipment has induced some criticism of policy. Unlike the U.K., Norway still has a considerable amount of attractive acreage left to offer. Only 20 per cent of the area south of the 62nd parallel has been licensed and its area north of 62 degrees—which many regard as the most promising acreage still unexplored in the non-communist world—is six times as large as that south of the line.

be taken without killing off incentive for further exploration or development is clearly much greater than that in a country which needs to stimulate employment and indigenous energy supplies. At the time of the first two licence rounds, the North Sea was still an unknown quantity at a time when the world's need for new energy sources and the world price for oil was still low. At the time of the third round, in 1969, interest was falling off in the southern sector in view of the lesser remaining structural prospects and the low price paid for gas. By the time of the fourth round in 1972, while the size of the round may well be considered too large, it could still be said that knowledge of U.K. prospects were severely limited and that, considering the problems which had arisen in the Middle East, Britain's need for oil was all the more urgent.

A more effective method of ensuring the maximum economic rent may well have been to auction from the start, or at least once it was clear that it was a highly prospective basin. But the discretionary system adopted by the U.K. did ensure, to a surprising degree, that U.K. interests gained a larger share of reserves by awarding them better blocks than they would have gained under alternative systems or by acreage alone. Of the 15 commercial fields under development in early 1977, U.K. companies (prior to participation) held 40 per cent compared with less than 20 per cent of the acreage allocated in the first four rounds, while the share of gas reserves in the southern sector amounts to about half compared to a similarly low proportion of acreage at less than 20 per cent in the first licence rounds.

The emphasis given by officials to the question of well commitments, which was the main competitive element in the first four rounds, has, on the evidence, resulted in a more sustained rate of drilling than might otherwise have occurred, particularly in areas such as the Celtic Sea and probably the North Sea in recent years as well. The deliberate intention to give extra weight to companies with the resources to develop fields and with refineries in the U.K. to use the oil has been largely fulfilled in that the major fields are largely in the hands of the international oil companies.

Above all, Government was able, to a degree not fully recognised to-day, to add a considerable element of competition into exploration by making large licence round awards of small blocks and deliberately encouraging newcomers and exploration groups to enter the field and pick up some of the moderately attractive blocks. Had the acreage awards been limited in extent and had the major oil com-

U.K. Licencing Rounds

Round	Areas under offer	No. of blocks on offer	Approx. total area (*sq. miles*)	No. of applications	No. of blocks applied for	No. of blocks granted	Approx. area (*sq. miles*)	No. of companies	U.K. Participation in acreage awarded (%) Total	U.K. Participation in acreage awarded (%) Public sector	Minimum work Programme (*wells*)
First (1964)	North Sea	960	86,000	31	394	348	32,000	51	31[1]	4[1]	98
Second (1965)	North Sea Irish Sea English Channel	1102	90,000	21	127	127	10,000	44	41[1]	10[1]	44
Third (1970)	North Sea Irish Sea	157	14,000	34	117	106	8,000	61	38[1]	15[1]	48
Fourth (1971/2)	North Sea Irish Sea Celtic Sea West Shetland	437 (15 auction)	39,000	123 (31 auction)	286 (15 auction)	282 (15 auction)	24,000	213	43 (22 auction)	5·3 (7·7 at auction)	225 (none in auction)
Fifth (1976/7)	North Sea Irish Sea Celtic Sea Western Approaches English Channel West Scotland	71	5,600	53	51	44*	3,400*	65*	74*	56*	51*

**Provisional*   *[1]Including options and assignments*

panies in partnership with British interests been given a virtual monopoly, the pace of exploration and development might have been very different as the major companies responded to their own international needs. The lack of enthusiasm for oil prospects among companies like Texaco, Mobil and BP in the North Sea in the early years is a case in point while the role of the independents—often misunderstood—in inducing a sense of excitement and in finding reserves such as the Hewett gas field and the recent Mesa oil find in areas not regarded as prospective by the major companies should not be underestimated, even though some ran into difficulties in the development phase.

The weaknesses of the approach have already aroused considerable public criticism. In the first place, by awarding such large licence rounds, particularly in the fourth round, the Government gave away its opportunites for controlling the pace of activity and exacting higher terms as time went on, to take advantage of the increasing attractions of the North Sea to the international oil industry. The object was to gear up exploration again after the apparent fall in 1970/1. The extent of the licence round was such that the industry had difficulties in digesting the amount of acreage it got. It is doubtful whether a continuous series of smaller allocations would have slowed things down (although the political response to the finds might have induced delays on the next rounds as it did in Norway), while they would have resulted in more advantageous terms for the Government.

By separating the question of economic rent from the licensing arrangement, the Government gave itself as a hostage to political fortune. It may be that, had the price of oil not risen, the combination of 12·5 per cent royalty and 50 per cent corporation tax would have ensured a tax take which compared reasonably favourably with other countries. Certainly the PAC exaggerated the degree to which oil companies as a whole would have been able to evade North Sea tax with accumulated artificial losses built up in the Middle East.[6] The

---

[6] The Government's estimates at the time suggested that, while capital expenditure reliefs would mean little tax income in the early years, within five years the company would be receiving about £5 per ton against £4 a ton company profit on a large field and that, for every £1 rise in the price, the Government would get 56p against the company receiving 44p per ton. The offsets against Middle East tax (see chapter 2) were limited to U.K. based internationals, and discussions were already taking place with the companies to stop this in mid-1972. This still left the question of corporation tax offsets against other parts of a company's

(*Continued on page 114.*)

failure of the British authorities to understand the nature of the oil industry at the time, with its profit base in the producing end, and its failure to understand the need for the public to see that justice was being done, was grave. The discretionary system — with its negotiations behind closed doors and the natural alliance of civil servants and politicians against any public debate of policy when it can be avoided—did much to lay the groundwork for its critics.

Successor Governments, because of this separation of elements of tax and licensing and because of the degree to which acreage in the North Sea had already been allocated, felt impelled both to act retrospectively to improve control, tax and national participation on existing fields and to pursue these aims in parallel rather than as a single package with the introduction of the Petroleum Revenue Tax, the passing of the Submarine and Pipelines Bill, the creation of the British National Oil Corporation and the negotiation of "voluntary" participation in existing finds.[7]

The question is now whether the U.K. has managed to do this effectively, despite the delays in North Sea production build-up which the prolonged negotiations helped to cause. It is a question which can not be answered confidently in the affirmative.

The introduction of a much altered Petroleum Revenue Tax, after the intense negotiations to round the edges of the original blunt proposals, is the element of Government policy which has aroused most relief and praise amongst North Sea participants and their bankers. Given the nature of the original proposals, which would have set a flat rate that would have badly discriminated against smaller higher cost fields and effectively killed off much of the explo-

---

(*Continued from page 113.*)
operations in the U.K. (refining, transport etc.), which might have been sizeable. The Government almost certainly underestimated the potential company returns on large fields from its existing tax structures. Elsewhere in the world, oil production was largely treated as a profit centre in its own right and taxed as such. State participation, as introduced by the Norwegians in 1969, would have taken the edge off some of the potential profit of companies and hence reduced incentive. But it does not alter the rate of return, in that the state pays its own share of costs. It was thus quite acceptable to most of the industry—and indeed attractive to some companies without the resources to develop fields on their own, although less attractive to the major companies which wanted the oil themselves and the largest possible cash flows.

[7] The major criticism at the time was levelled by Lord Balogh—see both his speeches in the Lords and his two articles in the *Banker* (March and September 1974). The justification of Government's policy of retrospective change was forcefully stated by Edmund Dell at the *Financial Times'* Scandinavian and North Sea Conference of 1st September, 1975.

ration effort, the final act has undoubtedly much to recommend it.[8] While the original concept of a single rate tax (45 per cent) imposed as a prior charge to Corporation tax and levied on a field-by-field basis has been maintained, a capital "uplift" provision of 75 per cent has been allowed (in other words 175 per cent of capital expenditure in a given period) has been allowed before profits are assessed. Greater flexibility in the system has been added by introducing both a ceiling on the rate of the tax (affecting large as well as small fields), a safeguard provision relieving fields of tax if rate of return fall below a defined level, a half-year allowance equivalent to 500,000 tons (1,000 barrels per day) before the tax becomes due and a discretionary ability of the Government to reduce royalties.

The effect of these changes has been to make PRT relatively attractive to companies in that (unlike the Norwegian system of both corporation tax and the Special Tax introduced at the same time as PRT) the companies gain a speedy repayment of costs before the tax combination bites and that the incidence of tax does vary between high-cost and low-cost fields. While the overall tax take in the U.K.—royalties, corporation tax and PRT—is estimated at around 70 per cent, it is likely to vary considerably between fields.

PRT nonetheless remains a remarkably cumbersome tax (the Norwegian system, producing a similar per cent take under present asumptions is much simpler and far more of a "excess profits" tax). It was based on an original concept introduced for adminstrative ease (a single tax levied essentially on cash flow rather than excess profits with some defined allowable costs) which was successively modified as the problems of incentive and low-cost producers were recognised by Government.

As such PRT remains rather insensitive to changes in price, costs

---

[8] For a more detailed discussion of the tax question, see *The Taxation of North Sea Oil*, papers and summary of a conference held by the Institute for Fiscal Studies on 12th February, 1976; Alexander G. Kemp's *The Taxation of North Sea Oil*, University of Aberdeen North Sea Study Paper no. 11, August 1976 and A. G. Kemp's *Taxation and the Profitability of North Sea Oil*, Fraser of Allander Institute research monograph no. 4, 1976. The drawbacks and criticisms of the Government's early proposals on tax during the first stages of the bill were discussed by E. E. Monteith of the International Energy Bank and others at a *Financial Times'* North Sea conference in London, 12-13th December 1974, while both the Norwegian and U.K. Government views on the tax were explained at another *Financial Times* conference in Oslo, 1-2nd September, 1975. Once again, the alternative forms of tax that might have been introduced barely seem to have been considered within the Government at the time and the options were certainly never opened up to public debate.

or delays which might be suffered. It does little or nothing to make a marginally commercial field less marginal, however far the incidence of PRT is eased. Relief from royalties may do more although this is disputed by some companies, which point out that royalties, which are set against PRT and corporation tax are rather less effective than they appear at first glance. Equally, PRT, may still be vulnerable to later political pressure in that it allows companies a period of very high cash flow before the tax bites. Forties, for example, is expected to have a net cash flow of over $1bn. in 1977 with a negligible PRT incidence (although this will quickly reverse itself in the following years) and similar figures can be seen for Piper before the situation tightens with high PRT payments—a picture which may well arouse new accusations of oil industry profiteering.

The presence of attractive terms for repayment of capital before tax burdens become due has also meant that the Treasury has kept to its determination to levy tax on a field-by-field basis rather than letting companies prolong the period before which tax becomes due by incurring new expenditure on other fields.

For the present, these defects may not be major. However should the present pause in new developments not recover as sharply as the country might wish, then the insensitivity of PRT to marginal field problems and the lack of encouragement it offers to companies to keep putting money back into new North Sea development could prove a much more severe drawback. PRT may be a masterpiece of political compromise and official ingenuity, but it is neither a simple nor a truely responsive additional tax.

The doubts whether Government policy is able to cope with changing circumstances, as officials and Ministers pretend, extend even more to the other areas of North Sea policy—controls and participation. In the Petroleum and Submarine Pipelines Act, the Department of Energy has taken extensive powers to intervene in depletion rates and exercise a discretionary control over new field investment. As a residual power, these may reflect a degree of commonsense, but so far there has been no statement of how the Government wishes to use them. Its present approach is based on a belief that governments should have as much discretionary power as possible to react to developments in the future. Its present re-assurance is simply that Governments will always act sensibly and in the best national interests.

The history of energy policy and civil service intervention in industrial questions is hardly an inspiring one and the British tradition of adjusting policy behind closed doors on a discretionary basis is far from ennobling.

One of the major weaknesses of U.K. licensing policy to date has been the lack both of debate and of policy definition surrounding it. Full discussion of depletion policy in public may not necessarily produce a better policy but it would at least ensure some critical debate about assumptions and concentrate the issue on broad aims. Leaving the question to be decided on the basis of individual decisions by officials about each field on an *ad hoc* basis leaves the door open to precisely the kind of short-term intervention without regard to longer term implications which has bedevilled British industrial policy since the war.[9]

The tendency to concentrate on means rather than ends is seen all too clearly in the development of participation and in British National Oil Corporation. Both developments, of course, arise from vague political commitments of the labour Government in 1974 and the peculiar political period of instability which followed. Participation has been an attempt to make sense of a Labour Manifesto commitment to take the North Sea into public ownership which has had to be pursued on a voluntary, "no loss no gain" basis. The BNOC has been the product of a similar commitment which has received less than enthusiastic support from some of the members of the Cabinet and a number of officials.

As it now stands, participation has become a contract giving the state rights to ownership of 51 per cent of oil and hence control over its final destination and, some say, in the operating and investment decisions of the companies concerned. It is a purely paper financial transaction which gives the state no real additional economic rent. The BNOC has meanwhile been built up as a potential owner of oil of very considerable significance, a supervising eye of Government in the operating decisions of companies, an exploration and operating company in its own right and a potential refiner, marketer and possibly, a petrochemical company.[10]

[9] See chapter 5.

[10] As of the summer 1977, BNOC stood to produce around 130,000 barrels per day as its direct share of oil production by 1981 and have access to a total of 1·2m. barrels per day (54 per cent of overall production) through its potential rights to royalty and participation oil (see Wood, Mackenzie report of June 1977). It has so far shown little desire to go downstream into refining and petrochemicals also in view of the market surplus. But its intention, announced in May 1977, of exercising all its participation oil options as they fell due, despite the low prices in the world market, is an indication of its determination to take an active role in the trade from early on.

As with the direct control mechanisms introduced by Government, the dual development of BNOC and participation in ownership of oil gives the state considerable powers to react to circumstances as they occur. If the lesson of the 1973/4 crisis is held to be—as some would argue—the direction of oil flows must be taken out of the hands of the major international companies during a time of shortage and if the central worry—is as some would think—that Britain's membership of the EEC will deprive it of many of its sovereign rights to control the flows and ownership of oil, then the discreet power which BNOC holds through its oil ownership could be of some considerable value. With its existing shares of oil production through its take-over of NCB's North Sea assets and Burmah's and its negotiated 51 per cent participation, it stands to have title to some 60 per cent of oil produced in the early to mid-eighties, when officials and Ministers consider a scramble for oil to be on the cards.

At the same time, it can also act as a national oil company in the sense of participating from the start in new licences, exploring on its own and integrating downstream in the manner which most other countries, consumer or producer, have sought. The imperatives behind this are varied. In part, as with other countries, they are emotional, stemming from the feeling that the public must not only gain a share of the proceeds of oil and some control of it—which it can do through tax and direct administrative regulations—but also be seen to be sitting on top of the commanding heights of the economy. In part too, the attraction of a state oil company lies in distrust of the motives and behaviour of the international oil companies and the determination to have a vehicle which can more closely check their activities and counter balance their decisions should the national interest require it.

The weakness of the approach is that the various aims, particularly those of control on the one side and of an entrepreneurial state oil company on the other, may not prove compatible. The Norwegians have strictly separated the roles between an Oil Directorate responsible to the Industry Ministry and Statoil. The Dutch have limited themselves to control and holding their share of production directly through the state. The experience of almost every country, especially Norway, is that a state company will quickly develop its corporate ambitions to grow and pursue monopolistic tendencies, whether by seeking more state investment than may be wise or by combining too closely with the international oil companies on tax and other questions, which will clash with the sponsoring Ministry.

In the case of the U.K., fears that BNOC may work in conflict with the national interest and pursue its own ambitions without effective definition of its role must be increased by the way in which it has been set up. On the one hand, it is growing quickly as a holding company of potential oil flows and is rapidly attempting, through participation, to become an oil company on the backs of the majors. On the other hand it has had enormous difficulty and some lack of interest in developing as a capable entrepreneurial exploration company in its own right.[11]

The result could be that it fails to achieve any real purpose. If one of the objects of a state company is to counter balance the interests of the international concerns and to undertake exploration and development investment which they would otherwise ignore because of their international commitments (particularly at a time when restrictions on new acreage awards and financial pressures may force out the competitive element provided by non-major oil companies, as seems to be happening in most countries), then BNOC seems ill-organised to do this. Indeed, to the extent that it insists on being commercial and acting in partnership with the major oil companies, it seems anxious only to repeat what can already be done by other companies and not to complement them by providing service areas which they are not willing to do.

Equally, its role as a supervisor of North Sea developments is greatly weakened both by its own corporate ambitions, which make it an interested rather than independent partner, and its human resource limitations. If Shell, with a total North Sea staff of around 600, is unwilling to take on more projects than it already has, then it is hardly likely that BNOC, with a quarter of this staff, can realistically supervise and contribute to operating decisions involving four or five times this work. Either BNOC will be tempted to intervene simply for the sake of self aggrandisement, in which case projects will be delayed for no useful purpose, or it will be tempted simply to let decisions go through on developments, in which case

---

[11] The potential contradictions between the company as a commercial concern and as an arm of Government have already been seen in the discussions about whether it should take responsibility for selling a drilling rig being built on the Clyde in 1976/7. The Corporation's determination to achieve a measure of independence of Government were illustrated in its raising of an independent loan of £825m. from U.S. and British banks in June 1977, with which it planned to repay most of the loans advanced from the Government's National Loans Fund. On the exploration side, BNOC has developed an ambitious approach to new acreage, urging allocation to it of licences outside the normal licence rounds.

its supervisory role will be minimal. In either case, it is difficult to see that the public interest is protected by its position as a 51 per cent shareholder in commercial fields.

BNOC may prove better than this. It may prove worse. On the evidence at present, there seems to be no definition of its functions and little structure to back them up. Its development would seem to depend on the aims and personality of those involved and to the extent to which the corporation is prepared to oppose Government and Civil Service.

7 The On-shore Impact

To an extent not always recognised, Britain is already enjoying—and has been for some years—the first impact of North Sea oil and gas. Since BP first announced plans to push ahead with the development of the giant Forties Field in 1972, capital expenditure on oil and gas fields in northern waters amounted to some £5bn. by the end of 1976 and was proceeding at a rate of more than £1bn. a year. In 1976 it accounted for a quarter of total U.K. industrial investment while over the period 1977 to 1985, it could add a further £8-10bn. to capital expenditure by industry. Total U.K. employment related to North Sea activities over recent years has amounted to around 100,000 jobs, more than half in Scotland. The impact of both the investment and job creation is believed to have changed quite strikingly the relative performance of Scotland as compared to the rest of the U.K. during the recent recession.

Not only has North Sea development proved to be one of the largest and most important new areas of industrial growth in the country since the war, it is also one that potentially at least, has stood to do much to ease the problems of decline in such traditional sectors as marine engineering and ship-building and to take British industry into a new and fast growing world market on the basis of a domestic market where much of the new technology and development has been tested.

It is a development which, because of its geographical location, could be held to have very considerable potential in reversing the traditional migration within Scotland from the north and north-east to the west central industrial belt, to revolutionise prospects within communities such as Aberdeen, the Moray Firth and Shetlands and to give Scotland a potential point of dynamic growth that could help counterbalance the decline of its traditional heavy industries and change its relationship with England.

Yet it is on nearly all these aspects that the response of British industry and the impact of North Sea development has so far proved extremely disappointing, especially when compared to the reactions of Norwegian industry and of industries in countries without off-shore production such as Belgium and France. The general response of British industry, with some notable exceptions, has been slow. The proportion of imported goods and services for the North Sea has, until recently, been extremely high at 60-70 per cent. The areas of high technology or skills such as off-shore installation, deep sea diving and platform design have been dominated largely by the U.S. companies with the major inroads coming from the French, Norwegians and Dutch rather than the British. The impact on Scottish and U.K. industrial performance, despite the high capital investment and its growth during a severe depression and over-capacity throughout manufacturing companies, has been relatively small.[1]

The argument from industry and Government has tended to be that the scale and speed of North Sea oil developments caught British industry and local authorities by surprise and that it was the size of the fourth round of licensing and the intensity of development programmes following it which were largely to blame.

This argument has an element of truth in it. The premium put by companies on guarantees of performance and delivery because of the high initial capital costs and the lead-times before production started has undoubtedly made them lean towards their traditional suppliers, particularly American companies, and away from U.K. companies.

What this argument leaves out is that, for five years, virtually the only real development in the North Sea took place in the southern part of the U.K. sector where over £500m. was expended on gas developments. It was here that the traditional techniques of the off-shore industry were first tested against North Sea conditions—with some disastrous results—and where the learning process for new-comers could have been used. Nor does it explain why other Continental countries were able to move in so quickly on platform design, especially concrete platforms in Norway, and installation once the development moved north—the more so when it is remembered that British equipment manufacturers, consultants and process plant contractors had been serving the oil industry for decades in the Middle East.

[1] To be fair to British industry, its reluctance to enter the market for fear that the long-term rewards would not be great could be said to have been borne out by the later experience of the dramatic fall-off in orders and surplus world capacity for rigs, services and platforms. Companies which did make major efforts to become involved in the market, such as Berry Wiggins in the U.K. and some of the Norwegian shipping and broking concerns have not had an easy time.

In fact, in the early years there were considerable efforts to get British industry involved. U.K. shipyards built twelve off-shore drilling rigs between 1958 and 1967, including three semi-submersible rigs. The traditional U.K. suppliers and contractors to the industry continued to do well out of the North Sea through the sixties, especially pump, valve and compressor manufacturers and contractors involved in the on-shore gas processing facilities. The gas era of the southern North Sea also saw the entry of a number of successful entrepreneurial companies, especially on the service side such as the Off-shore Supply Association operating supply boats and Bristow Helicopters.

But the early efforts to build-up a more extensive new entry into the off-shore fields (such as the North Sea Marine Engineering consortium of ten companies including Dorman Long and Cleveland Bridge founded in 1965 to build and operate rigs) failed.[2] The shipyards lost money on the first semi-submersible rigs and, unlike Aker in Norway (which lost money on its first rig and went on successfully to design and build its own) turned back to the then booming trade in oil tankers. The newly nationalised steel industry was able to get only a minute proportion of the undersea pipe laid for gas.[3] Virtually all the platform design and installation work was carried out by the major U.S. contractors such as Brown and Root and J. Ray McDermott.

When the oil developments came in 1970-1972, British industry, hard-pressed by the recession and falling profits, greeted them with a good deal of suspicion. The traditional oil suppliers and the entrepreneurial service companies (some of which had moved to other parts of the world such as Canada and Australia to keep their boats occupied during the fall-off in North Sea demand during the late 1960s) took steps to expand. Two important consortia—Laing-ETPM at Teeside and Brown and Root and Wimpey at Nigg Bay in Scotland—were formed to build platforms for the Forties Field. Much of industry was however, nervous of the high capital costs of

---

[2] See remarks by Ian Macartney of Amoco and "Monty" Pennell of BP quoted in chapter seven of Clive Callow's *Power from the Sea* (1973).

[3] In its evidence to the sub-committee on sea-bed engineering of the Select Committee on Science and Technology in 1974, British Steel said that it did not find the North Sea an attractive market in the early years and it revealed it had supplied only some 20 per cent of the sub-sea pipe used in the southern North Sea and none of the oil pipe used in the northern North Sea. Report of the Committee, *House of Commons 313, 1974.*

setting up facilities for the North Sea and of the cyclical nature of a market in which only a worldwide presence could protect a company. By the time companies did begin to prepare themselves and the Government had commissioned a report from The International Management and Engineering Group of Great Britain (IMEG) to point out the potential and define the important gaps, companies were already being caught up in the worldwide boom of 1972-4 and the new Conservative Government's policies of "go-for-growth".

When IMEG reported in 1972,[4] it estimated that U.K. companies had gained a share of around 25-30 per cent of a market then worth around £500-600m. per annum. Two years later when the Offshore Supplies Office, set up within the Department of Trade and Industry in response to IMEG's recommendations, reported, the U.K. share of a market in which the orders placed totalled £1·28bn. had risen to 40 per cent. The British share of traditional areas such as power generation equipment and pumps was over 80 per cent and its share of services such as helicopter, inspection testing and chemicals was over 60 per cent. The ability to build steel platforms was also high with four yards, and U.K. companies had built up considerable capacity to build modules for the platforms.

Nevertheless, in the key areas of off-shore installation, construction of concrete platforms (then beginning to take over from steel) and rig hire and pipelaying, its proportion was less than 25 per cent and in some cases less than 10 per cent. British Steel was unable to supply any of the large-diameter, high specification pipe required for under-sea pipelining. Much of the technology and design remained foreign (all the construction consortia had foreign partners for this purpose). The switch in emphasis from steel to concrete had caught the country unprepared, with delays in planning procedures for the few deep-water sites available around the U.K. and relatively few British designs approved by the industry. Of the 26 platforms ordered for

---

[4] "*Study of potential benefits to British industry from off-shore oil and gas developments*," by IMEG, HMSO, published January 1973. IMEG strongly recommended setting-up a semi-autonomous Petroleum Supply Industries Board. The Department of Trade and Industry's objections to this arose partly from classic civil service dislike of outside bodies and partly from the feeling that an internal Whitehall group would be more effective in ensuring government aid and muscle. To the extent its role that has primarily been one of persuading companies to buy British, this may have had some validity. But it has equally led to an obsessive concern with proportions of market, which have more political attractions, and has weakened its use as a constructive force in promoting investment and capacity.

northern waters by the end of 1974, 12 had been ordered abroad. And this in turn panicked the Government into introducing new regulations to speed up planning permissions and to put a potential £27m. into subsidies and guarantees for two sites to meet the expected continuing boom in orders[5] and to make strenuous efforts to try and create consortia to fill in the gaps of off-shore installation work.

The record of British industry's performance was far from good. All the British platforms were delayed by as much as a year and in one or two cases by two years.

A succession of labour disputes hit all the platform construction yards and many of the module manufacturing companies. At least one company, Occidental, switched its next platform order (for the Claymore Field) abroad as a result. Sir Frank McFadzean, then Chairman of Shell, was induced to declare bluntly in a speech during the summer of 1975 that his company's initial experience was that modules could be built twice as fast on the Continent as in Britain; that, despite efforts, it had been unable to find British yards willing even to quote to build the company's new semi-submersible and pipelaying barges; that platform construction in the country had been marred by poor productivity and labour disputes and that the Government's efforts to build up capacity in the Clydeside for employment reasons was "proving to be something of an albatross around the necks of the contractors".[6]

Even the City, which might have been expected to react more quickly to the demands of the oil industry for funds, seemed at times slow to appreciate the off-shore potential in the market. The insurance industry did exceptionally well. The banks—with a few notable exceptions amongst the merchant banks like Warburgs and Morgan Grenfell, and in the case of National Westminster—proved unwilling to set up the expertise necessary to review proposals and were nervous of the potential risks involved in the project finance which the smaller, and even some of the larger, companies wanted. BP had considerable difficulties funding more than 30 per cent of its Forties Field loan in sterling and, by 1975, it looked as if only some

---

[5] The sites are at Portavadie and Hunterston in western Scotland. By the summer of 1977, both had been prepared against considerable local environmental opposition, but neither had yet received an order. Nor were they likely to.

[6] *North Sea Oil—Climbing the Learning Curve*, address to the Scottish Business School Seminar, 13th June 1975.

20 per cent of total finance would be coming in sterling through British banks.[7]

Over the last few years, there has been a noticeable improvement in British performance, at least in its share of the market. The latest figures from the Offshore Supplies Office, for orders placed in 1976,

Analysis of Orders Placed by Offshore Operating Companies in 1976

	Value of orders placed	U.K. share*	
	£m.	£m.	%
Capital goods			
Fabrications			
1. Production platforms: concrete	25	22	88
2. Production platforms: steel	57	40	70
3. Modules and other fabrications	116	62	53
Production plant			
4. Power generation equipment	10	8·5	85
5. Pumps	5	5	100
6. Compressors	5	3	60
7. Process plant and equipment	18	16	89
8. Pipe	15	5	33
9. Pipe coating	17	17	100
10. Pipe fittings	10	7	70
11. Casing	54	46	85
Miscellaneous			
12. Communications equipment	12	10	83
13. Wellhead and completion equipment	9	5	56
14. Safety equipment	6	5·5	92
15. **Total**	359	252	70

[7] Part of the reason for the high proportion of loans in foreign currency was undoubtedly the greater attractiveness of terms for dollars. But the British banks could also be said to have proved slow to take an interest in the market and reluctant to set up the necessary expertise in petroleum engineering and other fields (a general criticism of U.K. banks also made by other parts of British industry). The same could also be said of the British equity market. U.K. investment companies were reluctant to participate with the notable exception of Oil Exploration in the early rounds). Since the fourth round, the interest has been much greater and the North Sea has proved one of the few areas where substantial risk capital has been raised through consortia such as L.A.S.M.O. The Stock Exchange remains opposed to allowing high risk share issues for exploration, partly because of a lack of confidence in its own ability to supervise them. The result—in contrast to the U.S.—is that the ordinary investor has found it difficult to take a stake in exploration and, forced into the secondary market, has not been shielded by any authoritative body such as the American Securities and Exchange Commission.

	Value of orders placed £m.	U.K. share* £m.	%
Services			
Exploration and drilling			
16. Rig hire (Exploration) and production drilling	105	27	26
17. Surveys	14	9	64
18. Drilling tools and equipment	13	7	54
General services			
19. Pipe laying	100	27	27
20. Installation operations	131	45	34
21. Diving	22	13·5	61
22. Helicopter and air services	20	12	60
23. Marine transport	56	22·5	40
24. Mud logging and well testing	8·5	3·5	41
25. Barytes and mud chemicals	13·5	9·5	70
26. Cementing services	8	4	50
27. Inspection testing and maintenance	12	8	67
28. Other services	92	80	45
29. **Total**	595	268	45
30. Design and consultancy	87	71	82
31. **Grand total**	1,041	591	57
Less			
32. Value of orders placed in areas where there is little current U.K. capability (8, 19, 20)	246	77	31
33. Performance in areas of U.K. capability	795	514	65

*U.K. share is the contribution to the contract value of U.K. labour and materials
Source: Off-shore Supplies Office, 1977

suggests that, of total orders of £1·04bn. the British content was £591m. or 57 per cent. The U.K. share of the capital goods side, which accounted for about half the value of total orders, rose from 47 per cent in 1974 to 70 per cent in 1976 largely because of a higher share of modules and steel platform orders. Its share of the services side also rose from 29 to 45 per cent over the two years, partly because of the development of new British capacity (generally through international consortia) in rig operations, platform drilling and pipe installation. The performance of U.K. platform yards has gone up, especially in the steel construction yards although the

Clydeside problems remain. There has been a noticeable effort by the larger industrial companies such as constructors John Brown, General Electric, British Oxygen and Taylor Woodrow to set up energy divisions and to extend their range in association with foreign companies.

The bleak picture now facing industry is that capacity has been built up and interest generated just as the off-shore market has begun to nosedive. The pace of new orders began to slip between 1974 and 1975, fell sharply during 1976 and is expected to fall again in 1977 compared to the 1974 peak, although there will be some recovery from the 1976 low. Actual expenditure has been sustained rather better because of the lead times between ordering and expenditure and continued to rise to a peak of £1·5m. in 1975 and £2bn. in 1976. Due to the pause in new field developments, it is likely to dip sharply in 1977 and 1978 in real terms and, even with some recovery in 1979 because of orders placed in 1977 and 1978, will need a dramatic pull from new field developments and discoveries if it is not to decline again sharply through the early eighties.

The difficulties which this downturn could bring are seen most obviously in the platforms sector. Against a theoretical capacity to build more than a dozen platforms at a time (more realistically around 10 a year since the larger platforms can take around 2 years to build) and planning permission for four more sites; and against official Government projections made in 1973 that the platform requirement in the northern part of the U.K. sector might amount to 5-13 per year in the following ten years, there have only been two new orders so far since the end of 1974 and only a further four to six platform orders are now expected during 1977 and the first half of 1978—enough at best to fill half the available berths and even then leaving some of them with a period of up to a year without work before the orders come. This picture could be changed by a sudden surge of platform orders for nearly all the dozen or so fields now discovered but not yet declared commercial and needing perhaps 15 platforms altogether. But, on present trends, this is unlikely. Nor will it do more than simply postpone the agony for a few years. On a more gradual path, around 5-6 platforms a year might be required, enough to keep the more successful yards in work but insufficient to keep the less successful yards busy or to ensure any payback at all for the money spent by Government in subsidising two additional yards.

The slow-down in platform ordering—which accounts for up to

20 per cent of the cost of a field development—must have its impact not only on the extensive module manufacturing capacity in the country but also on orders for machinery (pumps, valves, compressors, etc.) and for services associated with developments. Even with a new trunkline for gas, the pipelaying requirement over the next five years is unlikely to reach half the 15,000 kilometers laid so far.

Already there have been closures and lay-offs not only in platform fabrication yards but also in ancillary operations such as pipecoating. There are indications that the push given by North Sea expenditure to British industrial investment and employment generally is beginning to slacken, more especially in regions of Scotland and the north-east of England where the impact of North Sea work has been most pronounced.

The dilemma posed to the Government by this is uncomfortable. On the one hand, the Department of Energy may feel some relief that a slower pace of development eases its decisions on depletion controls. On the other, it is only a sustained and substantial development investment which—for all the argument about moderating investment in order to give British industry more time to cope—can provide any real push to employment and capital expenditure. After the development phase is over, there will still be a continuous degree of oil industry spending on maintenance. The Forties Field, for example, will require around 700 people to run it through its life. Total expenditure on operation and maintenance costs could run at around £600m. per annum through the first half of the 1980s for all fields, sustaining a substantial proportion of employment currentrently devoted to serving the off-shore drilling and installation facilities. On top of this, there should be at least a moderate extent of new field development through the period inducing expenditure of around £500m. through the period.

The 700 people required to run Forties compares with 7,500 required to build and install the equipment during the major investment phase, while the £100m. annual expenditure which may be required to run the Brent oil and gas facilities compares with four to five times this amount spent by the company during the years of peak installation.[8]

---

[8] Wood, Mackenzie and Co., one of the few organisations to estimate operating costs, suggests in its report of June 1977 that they could climb from towards $500m. in 1978 to an average of around $1·3bn. a year through the mid-eighties, compared to a peak capital expenditure of over $5bn. in 1976.

North Sea Impact

One hope when the oil developments first started was that the boost given to British industry on its own doorstep would encourage it to develop technology and capacity which would then be applied to the world market for off-shore goods and services—now running at some £6bn. a year, of which about £2·2-2·5bn. is in the North Sea, including the Norwegian and Dutch sectors.

But it is here that there must remain doubts. For all the improvement in U.K. shares in the British North Sea market, most of this, and the employment which comes with it, has been in areas of low technology such as construction of platform building facilities, pipe-coating, module construction and direct supplies to platforms and rigs. The figures do not distinguish between U.K.-owned companies and the subsidiaries of foreign companies and the concentration of policy and effort has tended to be on filling existing gaps rather than, as the Norwegians have done, building up world wide experience and capacity in particular areas of speciality (in the Norwegian case on rig ownership and operation and platform and equipment design).

There have been companies able to develop worldwide on U.K. experience, Weir Pumps in Scotland is an example of a group previously devoted largely to the marine industry switching emphasis to off-shore oil and gas facilities. The electronics industry, notably Plessey and General Electric, has developed advanced technology for communications and monitoring off-shore. The Vickers group is a rare example of a company which early on made major investments in advanced submersible vessels for off-shore work, using experience of telephone cable laying across the oceans. William Press is an example of a contractor which has turned its investment deliberately onto the off-shore oil and gas market.

The efforts to get into the key areas of off-shore rig and barge contracting, as even the Norwegians have found, may well have come too late in view of the worldwide surplus of equipment now estimated to last into the 1980s. British Government efforts, by the Offshore Supplies Office, to intervene on the positive side of new capacity creation have been notable more for their failures than their successes and the investment in Research and Development, while better co-ordinated than it once was, is still small by international comparisons and subject to the criticism of being too orientated towards relatively cheap research rather than the more expensive but more important development of new systems.[9]

---

[9] (*See facing page.*)

Much of the technology in the North Sea is still imported. The concrete platforms are almost all being made to foreign designs (e.g. Condeep, Sea Tank and Doris) as are the steel platforms (Brown and Root, J. Ray McDermott, ETPM), so that there may be only limited opportunities for the British side of international partnerships to gain orders from markets abroad. The figures produced by the OSO still show British industrial involvement as weakest in the most internationally moveable markets such as pipe, casing, rig hire, pipe laying, module logging and testing, and drilling tools and equipment.

This may be unfair to individual companies but is a generalisation which fits with the picture of British industry, particularly on the engineering side, as one in decline, tending to concentrate more and more on low-value-added items with limited international appeal. Certainly there is little evidence so far that the North Sea has provided the U.K. with either an alternative market for the declining sectors of shipbuilding and engineering or has contributed to the development of a base from which an export drive can be launched.

Another area of North Sea related expenditure on land which the Government has been promoting vigorously is investment in "downstream" refining and petrochemical facilities. The argument is an obvious one which is being followed by virtually all producing countries, including Norway and the Middle East, as they pursue an upgrading of their basic export raw material.

Although there undoubtedly will be considerable investment in further processing facilities in the U.K., the potential may well again be limited by the timing. The drop in demand growth rates has caught Western Europe and the U.K. with a substantial surplus of refining capacity on its hands which is likely, on present assumptions, to last well into the 1980s. In the U.K., refining capacity is likely to be around 3m. barrels a day crude capacity in 1980 against an internal demand which is not expected to reach this level until the end of that decade. Western Europe will require new refineries

---

[9] By 1977, the OSO had committed itself to loans to the value of £1·8m. to four companies. Of these, one, Moira (Marine Oil Industries Repairs Ltd), a consortium company set up to provide sea-going repair facilities, collapsed altogether. A second company, Automatic Oil Tools, got into difficulties and was taken over. The other two companies have never been named, although both are believed to be in the shipping field. The limitations of the research and development effort, meanwhile, were clearly highlighted in the evidence to the Select Committee on Science and Technology, sub-committee on offshore engineering, in 1974.

before then, but again a surplus is predicted on current plans until at least the middle of the decade.

As long as this is so, the economic advantages of forcing North Sea oil into the British refining system in the hope of gaining advantage through the export of products are questionable. The dispute between the oil companies and the Department of Energy over how much oil they will refine in Britain has been prolonged. Despite some statements by the industry, the average North Sea oil is not unsuitable to the market under a normal distillation process. Although heavier oils are required for bitumens and lubricants, North Sea crudes break down to a fairly satisfactory fit to the U.K. demand pattern for fuel oils, gas oils and petrol and naphtha, although using North Sea oil may tend to produce a surplus of the gas oils and middle distillates.

Statements by Ministers, on the other hand, suggesting that the use of North Sea oil in British refineries would bring with it extensive investment in upgrading facilities at plants thereby producing more petrol and higher fractions seem equally misleading. The stronger demand for petrol which is changing the pattern of U.K. consumption towards the lighter end of the barrel and away from heavy fuel oils naturally favours North Sea oil rather than the other way around and the investment now taking place in further cracking facilities in British refineries would have probably taken place anyway in order to cope.

The argument over "keeping the oil at home"—aside from the political emotions surrounding the issue—really boils down to whether the advantages of shipping the oil abroad as crude and retaining a high proportion of Middle East oils in Britain—where extensive investments have already been made to process heavier oils and where the premium paid for low sulphur oils is low—outweigh the advantages of keeping the oil in Britain and trying to ship it abroad as higher-value products.

So long as the sulphur premium paid by Europe is high (it has recently been as high as 50 cents to $1 per barrel) and as long as there is surplus refining capacity in Europe, which depresses the profit in processing, the advantages seem to be in exports as crude oil (particularly as freight rates for product carriers are higher than for crude carriers). Any additional refining capacity in Britain would have to be based—as the Nigg refinery proposal in Scotland is aiming for—on exports of products to the U.S., which present their own difficulties.

There may be more reason to hope that the North Sea may induce a more extensive investment in petrochemicals than might otherwise have been the case. The production of associated gas from the northern North Sea will bring with it substantial volumes of natural gas liquids, particularly ethane which is used extensively in the U.S. as the basic raw material for ethylene manufacture (the other two liquids, butane and propane, have more limited use as a petrochemical raw material). Already Exxon has announced plans for a major plant based on the new raw material, while BP/ICI also has plans. The Chemicals Economic Development Committee, which represents companies and unions in the industry, has suggested that Britain could increase its share of incremental petrochemical growth in Europe by as much as 10 per cent, involving the building of four new ethylene crackers by 1985, partly because of the advantages offered by access to secure raw materials.

But there are again limits to the extent to which the U.K. can displace existing plants in Europe through access to raw materials alone without depressing prices and thereby losing the economic advantages of doing so. While petrochemicals are predicted to enjoy a substantial growth over and above general g.d.p. in Europe, their rate of growth is beginning to moderate as their ability to substitute for other materials lessens. There is a surplus, on present plans, likely to exist in European capacity for some years and the raw material in the U.K. case is being landed well away from the major markets. The real advantage in petrochemical manufacture comes with the further processing facilities from ethylene. Yet—as the Norwegians have found with their petrochemical plans—the prices gained in the European market are not highly attractive.

Until a time comes when raw materials are in such short supply that access to them gives a company or country decisive economic advantages, or unless they are provided at extremely low prices (which seems unlikely given the cost of their transport to the shore in the North Sea), the development of an indigenous processing industry based upon them must move at a gradual pace ruled largely by the willingness of export markets to absorb the product. Even if the development of petrochemicals occurred as rapidly as the Government now hope, its impact on employment would be relatively slight (even a complex petrochemical plant employs no more than a few hundred personnel) and its impact in promoting other industries using the output would depend on the basic productivity and marketing efficiency of those industries.

North Sea Oil Employment in Scotland by Region—Mid 1976

Region		Oil employment in: Wholly involved units	Partly involved units	All units	Change since 1974 Employment	%	Oil employment as percentage of total employment in region
		(1)	(2)	(3)	(4)	(5)	(6)
Strathclyde	Manufacturing	4,200	6,750	10,950			
	Non-manufacturing	100	400	500			
	Total survey	4,250	7,150	11,400	+150	+1%	1·1%
Fife	Manufacturing	2,000	250	2,250			
	Non-manufacturing	—	—	50			
	Total survey	2,000	250	2,250	+600	+37%	1·9%
Tayside	Manufacturing	400	150	500			
	Non-manufacturing	800	100	850			
	Total survey	1,150	200	1,350	+400	+39%	0·9%
Grampian	Manufacturing	1,050	1,850	2,900			
	Non-manufacturing	9,300	450	9,750			
	Total survey	10,350	2,300	12,650	+4,000	+47%	7·3%
Highland, Western Isles, Orkney and Shetland[1]	Manufacturing	7,300	50	7,300			
	Non-manufacturing	600	50	650			
	Total survey	7,850	100	7,950	+3,900	+96%	9·3%
Lothian, Central, Borders and Dumfries and Galloway[1]	Manufacturing	550	1,200	1,750			
	Non-manufacturing	450	150	600			
	Total survey	1,000	1,350	2,350	—650	—22%	0·5%
Total Scotland	Manufacturing	15,450	10,200	25,650			
	Non-manufacturing	11,200	1,150	12,400			
	Total survey	26,650	11,350	38,000	+8,400	+28%	1·8%

[1]Total estimated oil employment in the Lothian Region is 1,900 (0·6% of total employment in the region), in Central Region 400 (0·4%) in Highland Region is 7,450 (11%) and in the Island Areas 500 (2·8%) while the Borders and Dumfries and Galloway regions have only minimal oil employment

Source: The Scottish Office "Economic Bulletin", Winter 1977

These limitations on the ability of North Sea oil to promote employment and diversified industrial investment on-shore are seen most clearly when the relationship of Scotland's economic performance to off-shore developments is considered. It is in Scotland, after all, that the primary impact of North Sea investment has been felt most strongly and where the change should be greatest.

Figures provided by the Scottish Office early in 1977[10] suggested that, on the results of a series of surveys carried out by the Department of Employment and the Scottish Economic Planning Department, the total number of people employed in Scotland through North Sea work had risen from some 43-50,000 in the autumn of 1974 to 56-65,000 in mid-1976. Oil employment in partly involved companies stood at 11,350. Oil employment in wholly employed firms had meanwhile risen to 26,650. The remaining number were calculated on the basis of the multiplier effects on consumption.

The strongest impact, taking the numbers directly employed without the multiplier effect, was clearly on the Grampian and Highland regions, accounting for 7·3% and 9·3% of employment in these regions. The Department's figures suggest that there have been considerable affects on the traditional manufacturing areas of Strathclyde, where some 30 per cent of those directly employed by oil developments were concentrated and over 40 per cent of those involved in the manufacturing side of oil employment.

At the same time there is some evidence that the investment and the employment effects of the North Sea have enabled Scotland to ride the recession of 1974/6 rather better than the U.K. as a whole. During the first half of 1976, for example, industrial output in Scotland rose by just under 1 per cent above the level a year earlier compared to a slight fall in the U.K. as a whole. And this was largely explained by the better performance of the investment goods sector in Scotland—mainly in construction and earth moving equipment, industrial plant and steel work, scientific and industrial instruments, insulated wires and cables and radio and electronic components. Within the construction side too, despite a fall in public sector housing, the North Sea seems to explain a relatively better performance in private output and a less sharp fall than in the U.K. in private non-housing output.

Nevertheless, while North Sea activity may have eased the problems of recession in Scotland—certainly compared to its relative

---

[10] *Scottish Economic Bulletin*, number 11, Winter 1977

performance during the previous recession in 1970-2—it did not reverse the recession itself. Compared to total employment, North Sea related employment is still small at less than 2 per cent of the Scottish total, and barely over 1 per cent of employment in the Strathclyde region.

If the major problems in Scotland continue to be the decline of the old-established heavy industries of shipbuilding, engineering and to some extent the coal industry, it seems unlikely that the North Sea can compensate. Even within areas such as Shetland, the Orkneys, the Moray Firth and Buchan, recent studies by the University of Aberdeen[11] have concluded that the impact of North Sea oil on employment and incomes has probably been exaggerated and that it will only partially reverse the drift away of population in view of the continuing decline in fishing, farming and knitwear.

The decline may, indeed, be compounded by the fall in demand for new platforms and field equipment. While the relative performance of Scotland may have been helped in the early part of the recent recession, there are now distinct indications from both the Scottish Office and CBI surveys that it may be slower to pull back. The fall in marine engineering and shipbuilding orders and lower demand for process plant coupled with the hiatus in platform orders all seem to point to the rather less buoyant expectations of revival appearing in the winter 1976/7 surveys of the CBI than expressed in Britain as a whole. Of the total 38,000 directly employed on North Sea work in mid-1976, some 12,500 were employed in platform and module construction and a total of 25,650 were employed altogether in manufacturing (including platforms) sectors whose orders closely relate to platform orders. The number employed in services, although of considerable benefit in the Grampian region, amounted to only 8,100.

The figures suggest in the first place that the often promoted argument that development should have been slowed down in order to enable Scotland to cope better may be true in the sense that a lower level of employment and benefit might be sustained over a longer time. However, such argument can not be true in the sense of benefiting Scotland's comparative economic performance more—rather the reverse would be the case.

---

[11] Occasional papers in the North Sea study being carried out by the Department of Political Economy: *Prospects for the Shetland Economy; Prospects for the Moray Firth sub-region; Prospects for the Orkney economy; Prospects for the Buchan economy,* all by G. A. Mackay.

It is this that forms the strongest distinction between Scotland and Norway. Norwegian fears of rapid development partly stemmed from fears of the impact of the monetary and foreign currency flows and partly from the fact that Norway was already a full employment country with limited capacity to absorb new demand (although the marine and construction industries were able to move with surprising rapidity on both the domestic and export front). In Scotland, the direct impact of North Sea oil, even at a time of low capacity utilisation and declining alternative demands in the engineering and shipbuilding sectors, seems to have been fairly small. The difficulties of adjustment, even in localised areas such as Buchan, seem to be much smaller than local authorities have sometimes declared.

The obverse side of the argument, as some Scottish academics have not been slow to understand,[12] is that, if the direct impact is so small, then the only real way for Scotland to boost its economic performance is to take direct hold of the oil revenues and currency earnings. The argument is in some senses highly theoretical. One would have to weigh against the benefits of such a move the severe economic dislocation that might occur with full separation as well as the resulting actions of the Shetland and Orkney Islands, who have so far indicated that they would split from an independent Scotland.

If a restrictive policy towards development or the export of capital were adopted, as in Norway, that would still leave the problem of investing sufficiently well to create a new industrial base. To an extent, the Norwegians, with a reasonably balanced economy, have such options, and even they have found themselves with problems during the recession. Countries, like Scotland or the U.K. as a whole, with a declining manufacturing base do not have the same opportunities.

Nevertheless, if Scotland cannot expect much from the direct effect of North Sea investment, it is bound to look with increasing interest at its prospects with control over the financial benefits of North Sea production. On present production and price profiles, North Sea might be worth the equivalent of a third of Scotland's g.d.p. in 1980 and over a half of its g.d.p. in 1985 while the tax revenue from oil might be nearly equivalent to total public expendi-

---

[12] The best studies remain *The Political Economy of North Sea oil* by D. I. MacKay and G. A. Mackay (1975) and the recent fascinating if speculative *Scotland 1980, The Economics of Self Government*, edited by D. I. Mackay (1977).

ture in Scotland, at current levels, by 1981, and 50 per cent more in 1985.

Given this kind of carrot, the hopes of U.K. Governments that the demands for devolution can be appeased with a combination of slightly higher rates of public expenditure from the centre through the Scottish Development Agency and limited control over their affairs through devolution could seem over-optimistic. If it their economic benefits of North Sea oil that the Scots seek, they may not be satisfied until they have at least a share in the proceeds.

8 The Real Benefits

It was the overwhelming balance of payments imperatives of the U.K. which first impelled the British Government towards rapid exploration and development of its North Sea resources. It is primarily to the balance of payments benefits from the oil and gas discoveries that the country is now looking to help break out of its traditional pattern of loss of world trade, low investment and slow growth.

Yet, despite the central importance that the North Sea has begun to play in the economic outlook of the U.K., discussion and analysis of the potential magnitude of its benefits and the policy options they might bring have come surprisingly late. In marked contrast to Norway, where the Finance Ministry intervened in 1973 with a long and detailed report on the economic impact of North Sea oil and gas with strong recommendations that policy be changed towards greater conservation and a slower pace of development, the British Treasury produced some provisional forecasts of the balance of payments impact only in the summer of 1976, and then only in a three-page paper whose fundamental assumptions on price, production and non-oil trade assumptions were left unstated.[1]

Instead, the public has been treated (in recent months) to a growing crescendo of moral exhortation from politicians at various times suggesting that the North Sea opens the gates to a new and more glorious future, or that it is a limited asset which must not be wasted and indeed may have been mortgaged in foreign debt. The main estimates of its potential value have been published by brokers and economists, who have variously argued that its impact will be to

[1] "The North Sea and the Balance of Payments", article in *Economic Progress Report*, no. 76, July 1976. This has since been followed up by an article updating the figures, presenting them at 1976 prices rather than current prices and including a forecast of off-shore income and expenditure and g.n.p. value in *Economic Progress Report*, no. 89, August 1977. The Norwegians on the other hand have produced a regular series of parliamentary reports on activities and implications almost from the start. The major Finance Ministry contributions have been in *Report No. 25*, in the 1973/4 session and *Report No. 50* in the 1974/5 session on natural resources and economic development.

change long-term the rate of economic growth much for the better or that it alters little the basic desirability of import controls or monetary restrictions or exchange controls or industrial intervention. Generalisations about mortgaging of North Sea assets to foreign creditors, about strengthening sterling and about massive new tax revenues have been thrown about at will. There has been no central core of debate because the government itself has never made its position clear (although officials have considered the problems in inter-departmental committees recently) and there has been no clear view of the economic impact because the estimates so far have, inevitably, been speculative and theoretical.[2]

The divergence of views is in some ways not very surprising—although the tardy development of the debate in Britain may be. Oil and gas, by their nature, form a special addition to a country's resources. As the fear of a collapse in world oil prices has diminished and acceptance of the crucial importance of energy supplies to future economic growth has become more widely recognised, so the potential value of having indigenous oil and gas has become more apparent. Few today would question that the total value of the discoveries and production of North Sea oil and gas over the next ten years far exceeds the cost of the debts incurred over the last ten years.

---

[2] The most detailed estimates remain those made by Professor Colin Robinson and Dr. Jon Morgan in the *Effects of North Sea Oil on the U.K.'s Balance of Payments,* Trade Policy Research Centre, Guest Paper No. 5, 1976. Other estimates, besides the Treasury forecasts, have been made by The National Institute of Economic and Social Research (*National Institute Review,* number 79, February 1977, "Some aspects of the economy,"); by J. S. E. Laury and P. J. Warburton of the London Business School (*London Business School Journal,* volume 2, no. 2, summer 1976); by Paul Akinson of the University of Cambridge Department of Applied Economics, (*Economic Policy Review,* March 1977); by Phillips and Drew in their *Economic Forecasts* and by Wood, Mackenzie and Co. in their regular *North Sea Report.* The most optimistic assessment of the potential North Sea impact on U.K. growth rates has been put forward by R. D. Nightingale and D. W. McGregor of Hoare Govett (*Economic and Financial Implications of North Sea Oil,* circulated by Hoare Govett, December 1976), which suggests that the North Sea could raise growth rates in the U.K. by as much as 2¼ per cent per annum largely on the basis of the fillip it will give to investment rates throughout the economy. The most forceful argument for the continued need to lower the exchange rates and move dramatically to restore the fortunes of manufacturing industry, despite the impact of the North Sea, is made by Wynne Godley of the University of Cambridge in the *Economic Policy Review*), while the strongest argument for an "international monetarist" approach, allowing exchange rates to rise, is made by G. T. Pepper in W. Greenwell's Special Monetary Bulletin on the *Economic Implications of North Sea Oil,* July 1977. An anti-monetarist view by Michael Posner is in J. and A. Scrimgeour's *Quarterly Economic Review* of July 1977.

However, rather like an unexpected inheritance from an aunt, the long-term benefit of oil and gas production depends crucially on how it is used and what effect it has on the lifestyle of the recipient. Of itself, oil and gas exploration and production brings relatively little direct employment and economic activity within the host country, particularly one such as the U.K. which is a mature industrial economy with a population of over 50m.

For a time, it does provide a market for platform construction, rig equipment and some on-shore related work in terminals and further refining and processing plant. But even at their height, these activities are fairly small compared to total employment and output; and, because they are most intensive during the construction phase, they tend to last for only a short period.

The most direct economic benefit of oil and gas production are the value-added increment it brings to total national output. At a time of high oil prices, this—despite the high costs of off-shore production—could be considerable, particularly in the early stages when the build-up of output is rapid. But, since Britain has a mature industrial economy with a high output, the direct effect on the gross domestic product is considerably less than it would be in say Saudi Arabia or even Norway and the Netherlands.

More important, this benefit is felt most directly in the balance of payments impact, which is crucial in a country like Britain where a persistent balance of payments deficit has traditionally constrained economic policy, and in tax revenue, which is important in a country with persistent public expenditure restraints.

However, oil and gas reserves are finite. Eventually, whatever the time scale, production peaks and goes into decline, thus creating a problem of "re-entry" as the direct benefits fall off. So while, for a couple of decades, the country may enjoy large annual increments to its g.d.p. with a relief from its balance of payments constrictions and a sizeable tax income, it faces the ultimate question of what happens when the inheritance runs out.

For a country like Norway, with a small population, full employment before oil development and a potential oil and gas output greatly in excess of its internal needs, it is possible to look at the options of delaying this day as long as possible and controlling its impact in the meantime. For a country like the U.K., with a large population, a high political sensitivity to unemployment, a persistent balance of payments deficit, and a substantial internal requirement for oil and gas, the question of how long the oil will last and how best to prepare for its decline have appeared more real. Barely has the oil started to flow, than officials and economists have started to argue over whether its benefits can be used to tackle the underlying problems of slow growth, thus enabling the country to emerge from its oil era with a strong underlying economic performance, or whether it will be used to maintain a short-term rate of consumption which will accelerate rather than reverse the fall in world market share of British manufacturing industry through an artificially high exchange rate and further borrowings.[3]

The difficulties of balancing out these factors and setting grand policy thinking against the practical likelihood of what oil will do for the British economy can be seen in gas development. It is easily forgotten that, for nearly a decade, the U.K. has already enjoyed a steadily increasing flow of natural gas of considerable potential benefit in import substitution and addition to the national income. The 1976 Treasury calculations put the benefit to the balance of payments as high as £200m. in current price terms during 1972, building up to £1·2bn. in 1974 and then, because of the quadrupling of oil prices, moving rapidly to £1·8bn. in 1975 and £2·7bn. in 1977, or around 2·3 per cent of g.n.p. at that time (a proportion which is expected to continue throughout the rest of the decade).

There can be no doubt that the impact has been substantial, relative to what the balance of payments might have been without it. There is at least an argument that the current account benefits of gas have been sufficient to cover the heavy import of oil equipment during the last four years or so whilst its direct benefits in government revenues have not been large due to the low prices, and hence low taxes. There have nonetheless been benefits in lower gas prices paid by the consumer than would otherwise have been the case, a high investment and rapid depreciation of assets by the gas industry and a far from unrespectable financial performance by the state

[3] The political debate was launched in a series of speeches by Denis Healey, Chancellor of the Exchequer, and James Callaghan, the Prime Minister, from the Spring of 1977. A discussion paper on the options, expected to emphasise the need to preserve British industrial competitiveness, to develop alternative energy sources (particularly coal) and to suggest the establishment of a North Sea Fund to invest in job-creation in the developing regions and Scotland, was promised for the Autumn of 1977. This paper, discussed between the Departments of Energy, the Scottish Office and the Treasury, has been backed by an inter-departmental working party of officials, apparently set up in 1976 to look at the long-term use of North Sea benefits and the balance of payments implications.

gas concern, which might otherwise have proved a drain on the public purse.[4]

Yet, what the experience of the last few years has equally shown is that the broad economic impact of natural gas has been very far from preventing a deteriorating balance of payments, generally worse than that of other industrialised nations since the oil crisis of 1973/4, and a continuing deterioration of British manufacturing industry's performance in terms of its share of world trade. Unemployment has continued to rise and, to the man in the street, the impact of natural gas on his standard of life has barely been noticeable.

The cost of extracting oil from the North Sea, although considerably less than its present value on the market, is still on average rather higher than the cost of importing oil before the 1974 price rises when the import cost averaged around $3 to $3·50 per barrel. Considering that the resources required to produce the oil now are no less than those required to import it during the early 1970s, there would seem to be no absolute reason why Britain in the post price-rise era should enjoy dramatically higher growth rates than during that era.

The growth rates of competitor countries without oil may well lessen as a result of having to concentrate more resources on paying for high-cost energy imports. But, unless the U.K. exports a substantial amount of its oil surplus to its own requirements—which seems rather less likely than it once did in view of both the political pressures for depletion control and the slackening pace of development—the North Sea will do little more than recover the impetus lost because of higher oil and other commodity prices after 1974.

This would indeed appear to be borne out by the broad estimates of the added value wealth that oil will bring to the U.K. over the next ten years. Much will depend, of course, on the relative course of prices and costs (although the experience of 1974 would suggest that costs tend to rise rapidly at a time of oil price increases). Until

---

[4] The full extent of the benefit of the low purchase price of gas to the Gas Corporation has been disguised in recent years by the Corporation's changes in accounting policy towards depreciation on the basis of full replacement cost—a line it justifies by its need to prepare for higher-cost supplies and investments in the future. The relatively low price of gas to the domestic consumer meanwhile encouraged the Government to take the extraordinary decision to compel the Corporation to raise prices in Spring 1977, partly to enable B.G.C. to repay Treasury loans early and partly to meet the complaints of the coal industry about the competition from gas.

U.K. Income from Oil and Gas Production

(£ *billion at 1976 prices*)

	1976	1977	1978	1979	1980	1985
1. Oil and gas sold	1·0	2·7	3·9	5·3	6·0	7·5
2. Goods and services bought outside the "sector"*	0·1	0·2	0·3	0·3	0·4	0·6
3. Employment income	—	0·1	0·1	0·1	0·1	0·2
4. Total royalties plus profits before tax	0·8	2·4	3·5	4·9	5·6	6·5
5. *of which* interest, profits and dividends due abroad	0·1	0·6	0·8	1·4	1·7	1·2
6. GNP at market prices arising within the "sector" (equals line 3, *plus* line 4, *minus* line 5)	0·7	1·9	2·6	3·7	4·0	5·5

*Defined as operating costs less employment incomes

Source: H.M. Treasury, "Economic Progress Report", August 1977

1985, the North Sea can be expected to contribute something like 3-4 per cent to the U.K. g.d.p. in 1980, rising to 5 per cent in 1985, in terms of value added less remissions abroad. This is based on reasonably optimistic assumptions that the output will increase to around 2·5-2·8m. barrels per day in the early 1980s and that oil prices will keep pace with cost inflation over the next few years and begin to rise in real terms from the early to mid-eighties to around double by the end of the century (both assumptions contained in the recent report by the Department of Energy to the National Economic Development Council in early 1977).[5]

Because of the rapid initial build-up of production to around 2m. barrels a day by the turn of the decade, the impact of North Sea oil on annual growth rates will be greatest during the next few years, adding around 0·5-1 per cent per annum cumulatively to g.d.p. until 1980/1 (with the greatest impact being experienced in 1977, 1978 and 1979), and gas production adding perhaps a fraction more. After that, the calculations become more sensitive to the course of prices and production. If output levels off from the mid-eighties and prices rise in real terms, the annual increment will be rather slower at about 0·2-0·3 per cent per annum in the early 1980s, slowing down still further in the late 1980s and early 1990s.

Should the price of oil fall in real terms, there remains a considerable addition to g.d.p. over the next few years but it declines sharply from the early 1980s. If the price, as could happen, moves in fits and starts with a sizeable increase of perhaps 50 per cent in the

---

[5] There has been little attempt so far to make detailed estimates of the precise direct or indirect impact of the North Sea on g.n.p. or g.d.p. for the obvious reason of the uncertainties involved. Professor Robinson and Dr. Morgan give a broad estimate in terms of the potential balance of payments benefit as a proportion of g.n.p. (3-4 per cent in 1980 and 3-7 per cent in 1985). The "Cambridge Group" in the March *Policy Review* estimate total tax revenue and profits retained in the U.K. as a proportion of total national income, both direct (at a modest 3 per cent in 1980 and 3·7 per cent in 1985) and direct and indirect combined (2 per cent in 1976 rising to 6·5 per cent in 1980). Hoare Govett's December 1976 calculations, suggesting a potential boost of 2¼ per cent per annum to long-term g.d.p. growth rates, is based on a theory of the boost it will give to underlying investment rates. The Treasury, meanwhile, made an estimate of the net effect on the overall balance of payments of oil and gas as a percentage of g.n.p. (a combined 5 per cent in 1980 and 7·8 per cent in 1985) in its July 1976 *Progress Report*. The most recent *Report* attempts new calculations of the total direct income arising from the production of oil and gas offshore by defining it as a sector. It estimates a g.n.p. forecast at market prices within the sector but this is in terms of value (£4bn. in 1980 and £5·5bn. at 1976 prices) and is not estimated as a percentage of the total (although this implies a percentage of g.n.p. of around 3 per cent in 1980 and 4·5 per cent in 1985).

early eighties, the cumulative $\frac{1}{2}$ per cent addition to g.d.p. would be sustained through the early and mid-eighties. While sensitive to the price of oil, however, the order of magnitude of the North Sea contribution to economic growth still remains relatively moderate and would seem to be equivalent to the loss to growth which Britain's major European competitors expect to suffer as a result of high oil prices.

It is in the form of its contribution to the economy—in balance of payments relief, in direct revenue to Government and in its boost to private sector profits — that the real importance of the North Sea lies. By the summer of 1977, the build-up of output had done much to turn a trend of record balance of payments deficits in the previous two years to one of balance (including invisibles) on the current account.

Despite continuing high inflation and the worries over the future course of wage restraint in the country, the development of oil is making a major contribution to strengthening sterling, encouraaging capital inflows and building up foreign reserves. Its impact on the balance of payments is encouraging the Government to think of expanding the economy again in 1978 through tax cuts. And there are signs that the pessimists on the North Sea's economic contribution are underestimating its potential effect.

Exact calculations, as ever, are riddled with the uncertainties of price, production profiles, the behaviour of foreign oil companies in the repayment of capital as well as payment of dividends abroad, the non-oil impact of North Sea oil—or what the Treasury refers to as the "imports/exports displaced by North Sea programmes", as well as the effect of production on foreign currency reserves and interest rates.

The estimates made by the Treasury and by various economists, too, are necessarily based on assumptions of what the economy would have been like without North Sea oil in order to identify its potential effects. They are, thus, calculations of potential impact on the balance of payments, not predictions of how the balance of payments will perform—which will depend on other factors such as non-oil trade, repayment of debt and hence the size of interest payments, as well as the extent to which the economy is run at a higher level, inducing increased imports. Nevertheless, such calculations remain the only way to gain some idea of the order of magnitude of the balance of payments benefit of the North Sea.

If the production profile up to 1980 is virtually confined to fields currently under development and assuming that any slippage caused by delays in construction of the Sullom Voe terminal in the Shetlands will be largely compensated for by higher-than-predicted initial flows of other fields such as Piper and Forties, production of oil should climb quite rapidly to around 2-2·2m. barrels per day by 1980. The value should then be equivalent to around £6·8bn. at current prices (£5·6bn. in 1976 prices), depending on whether prices in real terms fall (quite possible considering the potential surpluses of supply in the next few years) or manage to keep pace with general world inflation rates of 5-8 per cent per annum. There will also be additional value from gas over and above existing supplies from the southern fields at perhaps £1·5-2bn. in current price terms.

The year 1985 is more difficult to estimate in view of the range of production profiles and assumptions on prices. Assuming that production builds up gradually rather than radically from existing discoveries and levels out at around 2·6-2·7m. barrels per day, and assuming that the price—whether it falls in real terms in the next few years or not—then rises at a sharper rate in the 1980s, the gross value of the oil in the mid-eighties could be around £14bn. or £15bn. at current prices (around £7·8bn. at 1976 prices). If production rises to 3m. barrels per day and prices keep up with inflation of manufactured goods, the figure might be higher by around £2bn. Equally if prices continued to fall in real terms and existing discoveries not already under development came in only gradually, then the gross value of oil could be several billion less at around £10-11bn. at current prices.

There could be additional gas if the major gas trunkline goes forward, worth perhaps £700m., while the value of northern North Sea gas from fields already under development would have risen to as much as £1·2-1·5bn.

Against these gross value figures—at current prices—there would be considerable offsets to the current account benefit as a result of imports of goods and services and repatriation of interest and dividends from U.S. companies. The precise figures are again difficult because they depend on the degree of capital expenditure expected, itself a function of inflation in costs and the extent to which new fields are brought into play, and the proportion of this expenditure provided by British companies. On a rough estimate that the total expenditure would begin to decline at the end of the decade as the slower pace of the second generation of development made a stronger impact, assuming that operating expenditure might approach £1bn. a year with inflation, and assuming that the U.K. share might rise to around 65 per cent, the import of goods and services, which in 1976 totalled some £1·2bn., might be expected to fall to below £1bn. at the end of the decade. Imports may then stabilise with inflation and new developments through the middle of the decade (although there is some argument that they could fall even further with a slow pace of new development or rise with a jump in the price of oil).

The remission of profits and interest payments abroad is even more difficult to assess, since much depends on how companies decide to amortise their loans and how hard the tax bites. If foreign companies owning around 60 per cent of U.K. oil reserves wish to repay capital as quickly as possible, interest, profits and dividends are likely to rise fairly slowly through the rest of the seventies to around £1·5bn. by 1980 and then climb rapidly afterwards as the investments are fully depreciated and, in theory at least, the full extent of profits is remitted abroad. So while loan interest may fall sharply through the early eighties, remittance of earnings could still climb as high as £2-3bn. by the middle of the decade.

The capital account meanwhile has so far been heavily influenced by inflows of oil company investment into the U.K. Most foreign companies appear to be raising their capital from abroad and U.K. companies seem, on current evidence, to be raising around 60 per cent of their North Sea funds in foreign currencies (even BNOC has recently raised its first major £650m. loan entirely on the dollar and Eurodollar markets). In 1976, the inflow was as high as £1·5bn. and could remain at this order of magnitude until 1979 before declining rapidly with the slower pace of development. Capital outflows will depend on company policies. Assuming a policy of rapid repayment, these could rise to around £1bn. by 1978/9 and stay at that level until around 1982/3 before easing off again.

The figures are necessarily imprecise at this stage but they do give some indication of the orders of magnitude and the degree to which the trade effect of North Sea oil and additional gas will quickly outstrip the debits on the North Sea current and capital account. Over the past two years (1975 and 1976), capital inflows largely seem to have matched the inflows of equipment and services for the North Sea, if not proving slightly higher than those imports.

During 1977, the position should turn dramatically as the value of oil output, particularly from the Forties and Piper Fields, begins to dwarf the capital expenditure and import figures. The net effect

Government Estimates of North Sea Impact

Potential U.K. Balance of Payments Effects of the North Sea Oil Programme

(*£ billion at 1976 prices*)

	1976	1977	1978	1979	1980	1985
1. Oil exports/imports saved (incl. insurance and freight)	0·7	2·3	3·4	4·8	5·5	6·7
2. Imports of goods and services for North Sea programme*	—1·3	—1·0	—0·9	—1·0	—0·9	—0·5
3. Imports/exports displaced by North Sea oil programme	0·5	0·5	0·5	0·6	0·7	0·1
4. Interest, profits and dividends due overseas	—	—0·5	—0·7	—1·3	—1·6	—1·1
5. Net interest on official assets/liabilities (as measured by the cumulative total of 1-4 and 7)	0·1	0·1	0·3	0·5	0·6	1·5
6. Net effect on current account	—0·1	1·4	2·7	3·7	4·3	7·6
7. Net effect on capital account	1·0	0·7	0·7	0·8	0·7	—0·1
8. Net effect on overall balance of payments	0·9	2·1	3·4	4·5	4·9	7·5

*The programme includes development, exploration and operating costs

Source: H.M. Treasury, "Economic Progress Report", August 1977

of North Sea oil on current account in 1977 could thus amount to £1·5bn. (a total effect of more than £2bn. on the balance of payments if the continued capital inflows are taken into account). From then on, the impact should rise by more than £1bn. each year until 1980 when the net effect on the current account should be about £5bn. to £6bn. at current prices (£4-4·5bn. at 1976 prices) rising to perhaps £10-£12bn. at current prices by 1985, or around £8-9bn. at 1976 prices.

This is on the assumption of a moderate price rise for oil in line with inflation and a further expansion of production from new fields. If that expansion is not forthcoming and the price of oil declines through the period relative to other prices, thus further curbing new development, the effect could be to reduce the balance of payments impact to £4·5bn. in 1980 and to £6bn. in 1985. If, on the other hand, prices rise continuously through the period in real terms and additional production is brought on at a more rapid rate than currently expected (to 3m. barrels per day or slightly more in the mid-eighties), the figures could go to £7bn. in 1980 and as high as £17bn. in 1985 at current prices.

In addition to this balance of payments impact—with all it implies for a release from traditional trade and reserve constrictions on economic growth, relief on interest rates on foreign debt and investment opportunities—the country can also expect substantial, although smaller, benefits to public sector revenue and national income. Royalty payments start from the beginning and, assuming a little over 10 per cent after expenses have been allowed, should grow from around £44m. (£66m. including gas) in 1976 to twice this amount in 1977, rising to about £800m. in 1980 and some £1·5bn. in 1985 at current prices, depending upon the rate of oil flows and prices. Corporation Tax and the Petroleum Revenue Tax will not bite until later because of the capital allowances, particularly for PRT whose impact will be most on the major fields under development rather than future higher cost fields. Together, with PRT accounting for perhaps 60 per cent of the total, tax revenues should amount to over £1bn. in 1979 and around £2bn. at current prices in the following year rising throughout the early eighties, although more gradually. This would give an annual tax take, including royalties, of around £3bn. at the turn of the decade and £5-6bn. per annum in the early to mid-eighties at current prices, or £2-2·5bn. in 1980 and £3·5bn. in the mid-eighties at 1976 prices.[6]

---

[6] (*See facing page.*)

The flow of taxable profits to British companies, directly from oil production and from related services and manufactures, is almost impossible to estimate with any accuracy. A portion will be taken up by the British National Oil Corporation which will almost certainly use it to re-invest, and the British Gas Corporation. The London-based internationals, Shell and BP, may invest part of their profits abroad, although both they and the U.S.-based companies are likely to re-invest a substantial proportion within Britain.[7]

In so far as the funds will boost income in the personal and corporate sectors, they are clearly important. Calculations made by the National Institute, the London Business School and the Cambridge Group suggest that post-tax profits of British companies might total as much as £1-1·5bn. a year in the mid-eighties.

Again, all these figures have to be put into some sort of perspective. The estimates of potential public sector revenue, at around £3-4bn. per annum in the early to mid-eighties at 1976 prices has to be compared with a current public sector borrowing requirement of £7·5bn. and total receipts of over £50bn. in 1976/7, and are unlikely to be more than around 5-8 per cent of total public sector income in the early eighties. The calculation of post-tax profits of British

---

[6] Revenue estimates are subject to even greater sensitivities of price, costs and output than balance of payments figures. The latest Treasury estimates, for a total revenue of £5bn. between 1976 and 1980, with a level of around £3·5bn. in the early eighties show a marked downward revision from the estimates of £5·5bn. between 1976-1980 and an income of around £4½bn. per annum thereafter "because of changes in the economic assumptions underlying the calculations." Most other estimates, by the Cambridge group, the London Business School and Phillips and Drew would put the revenue rather higher. Hoare Govett's estimates of direct revenue are reasonably in line with the Treasury's, but they estimate an additional revenue from corporation tax on supplying companies and income tax on employees as well as interest savings for the authorities which could more than double the figures.

[7] The early indications were that foreign-based companies such as Exxon and Amoco would spend a substantial proportion of their initial profits within the U.K., particularly on processing investment. BP has shown an aggressive desire to use some of its Forties Field revenues to build-up a stronger position in the North Sea through farm-ins and to acquire marketing companies in Britain. In the early to mid-eighties, however, the pressure on the multi-national companies to repatriate their profits for use elsewhere could become much stronger. The potential impact of the North Sea in the early stages, particularly when set against the current recession, can be seen from the economic indicators for early 1977. These suggested that one-fifth of all profits in the first quarter of the year came back from the North Sea and that off-shore development was responsible for increasing profit share from around 6½ to 8 per cent of g.d.p. At the same time the North Sea accounted for a quarter of all investment in industry during the two preceding years.

companies from North Sea developments of around £1-1·5bn. a year in the mid-eighties at current prices has to be set against total trading profits of all companies, net of stock appreciation, at £7·7bn. in a recession year of 1976.

The calculations of balance of payments benefit have to be related to a visible deficit of over £3·5bn. in 1976. Even on the more optimistic assumptions, North Sea production will be equivalent only to around 10 per cent or less of the total export of goods and services. Because the estimates are notional in the sense that they separate the North Sea impact from the trade performance as a whole, they tend to disguise the fact that the underlying trend in non-oil trade remains poor, that there is likely to be a sizeable deficit on capital account (due to export credits and remissions to foreign-based companies) and that trade surpluses are unlikely to be anything like as high.

Nevertheless, there can be no doubting the potential importance of the impact of North Sea on revenues and trade. Although foreign currency borrowings at present are high, partly in anticipation of the North Sea, even at the peak repayment schedule of $2·4bn. in 1979, $3·2bn. in 1980, $4.7bn. in 1981 and $3·2bn. in 1982 (as recently published by the Treasury), the potential balance of payments revenues of the North Sea are more than enough to cover the repayment, including an estimate for capital outflows for export credit and overseas investment accounts. After 1982, the gap between North Sea benefit and repayment becomes progressively wider by 2-300 per cent and more.[8]

More important, the timing and the nature of the benefits indicate possibilities for economic expansion and investment which were not there before. If balance of payments constraints have been one of the main obstacles to sustained U.K. growth, since expansion has always been followed by payments deficits leading to domestic deflation, the North Sea could at least provide an opportunity to ease this, giving British Governments an option either to repay debts and accumulate reserves or to allow the economy to run at a higher pace and allow more imports. If the public sector deficit has been a major worry, the tax flows could act on it. If it is lack of investment which has been the root cause of the low rate of British growth, then the lower interest rates and the monetary flows as well as

---

[8] The full schedule of repayments is published in an article in the May 1977 issue of the Treasury's *Economic Progress Report*.

Scheduled Repayment of Foreign Currency Debt of the U.K. Public Sector 1977-1986

($ *billion*)

	1977	1978	1979	1980	1981	1982	1983	1984	1985	1986
H.M.G. $2·5 billion loan	—	—	—	—	0·6	0·6	0·6	0·6	—	—
H.M.G. $1·5 billion loan*	—	—	—	—	0·2	0·3	0·3	0·2	—	—
I.M.F.—oil facility	—	—	0·2	0·3	0·3	0·3	0·1	—	—	—
—May 1976 drawing on 1st credit tranche	—	—	0·2	0·4	0·2	—	—	—	—	—
—January 1977 drawing on $3·9 billion standby	—	—	—	0·4	0·6	0·1	—	—	—	—
Foreign currency bonds	—	—	—	—	—	0·2	—	0·5	—	—
Long-term debt	0·1	0·1	0·3	0·1	0·1	0·2	0·2	0·1	0·1	0·1
Borrowing by other public sector bodies	0·0	0·7	1·7	2·0	2·7	1·6	0·8	0·6	0·1	0·1
Totals†	0·2	0·8	2·4	3·2	4·7	3·2	2·0	2·0	0·3	0·3

*Drawings up to end-March 1977 only

†Individual items may not add up to total because of roundings.

Source: H.M. Treasury, "Economic Progress Report", 1977 May

U.K. private sector profits which North Sea will bring could provide some of the urgent boost which the Government has been looking for.

Predictions that the North Sea developments will have a much more extensive impact on British economic growth—as high as 3 per cent per annum on some calculations—are based on the indirect multiplier effects that this balance of payments benefit could have and on the productive investment which it could promote.

It is the difference between the direct impact of North Sea development on British g.d.p., likely to be only moderate, and the opportunities for more sustained growth that this benefit might bring, with the added edge that the once-and-for-all benefits will begin to decline in the 1990s, which pose overriding questions.

The major impact of the North Sea for the public will tend to be in the earlier rather than the later years, as it acts on an economy only gradually climbing out of recession, as the optimism promoted by first impact encourages an inflow from abroad and as the first monetary flows, which could be extremely large, work their way through the system.

However, it will also be acting on an economy in which the underlying balance of payments is still in deficit; productivity does not appear to be improving as fast as it should; substantial foreign debts have been built up (some $19bn. is due for repayment between now and 1986 according to the Treasury); and the social and political pressures on wages, public expenditure and consumption arising from four years of restraint are very strong indeed (not to mention the pressures in Scotland for a more direct and larger share of the benefits).

If the underlying reasons for the U.K.'s poor economic performance were really as simple as a balance of payments constraint which prevented sustained higher growth through rising domestic consumption, or a lack of investment funds, or a "crowding out" of the private sector by the growth of the "non-productive" public sector, the trade and revenue benefits of North Sea oil could be expected to go some way towards reversing the situation.

The evidence suggests that the problems are more deep-rooted than this, and that the low investment per operative in U.K. industry, the decline of its manufacturing base and the high propensity of the country to import at times of growth, arise from more fundamental structured weaknesses reflecting a growing irrelevance of many of the major industrial sector's products to world demand; a concentration on lower value added products; poor productivity of British investment rather than lack of investment funds *per se* and a tendency to concentrate on short-term profits rather than long-term returns.[9]

The argument as to why this should be—whether lack of profits, structural weaknesses in the capital markets, overweaning union power and strikes, too rapid a public sector expansion, educational methods, or simply history—is one that has produced more disagreement than concensus as various macro-economic policies of exchange rate depreciation, public expenditure cuts, incomes restraint and domestic deflation in order to make room for export-led growth all seem to have failed to provide the solution.

There is nothing in the North Sea that can of itself, provide an answer to these questions. It is simply not large enough to cope with all the competing claims for higher real wages after the fall in real incomes over the last two years and the higher corporate profitability which the private sector demands, the larger investment in manufacturing industry which the Government is calling for, the improvements in education, health and other social services which politicians call for, and the investment in long-term alternative energy sources which the Department of Energy is urging. It can do one but not all.

Indeed, it may simply make policy decisions more difficult in that the disciplines of the economy will be correspondingly loosened. What the North Sea does is to give the Government a degree of option as to whether it uses the value of production to build-up reserves and repay debt (as recent Bank of England and Treasury statements suggest); attempt to encouraging continuing export growth through deflation at home and a low exchange rate; or, as others would argue, promote consumption, and hence investment, over a sustained period, with or without import controls to curb

---

[9] The problems of Britain's industrial decline have aroused great public attention and considerable analysis recently. A good deal of anecdotal evidence of the underlying weaknesses in manufacturing performance has come from the reports of the tripartite sector working parties on industrial strategy in 1976 and 1977 and the analyses done by the National Economic Development Office (M. Panic and A. H. Rajan's *Product changes in industrial countries' trade*, R. W. Bacon and W. A. Eltis' *The age of U.S. and U.K. machinery* and the *U.K. and West German manufacturing industry*) as well as the recent Government studies into the car and motorcycle industries. For a discussion of the difficulties of defining the causes of differing countries' performances, see also *Why Growth Rates Differ*, E. F. Denison, Brookings Institution, 1967.

the import propensity which has defeated such expansionary policies before.

Each course is fraught with difficulties. To use the main benefits in reserve accumulation, interest reduction and the repayment of debt would mean continuing to restrain domestic consumption and thus forego many of the immediate and medium-term benefits that might arise from allowing domestic consumption to grow more rapidly. The political tensions of such a course would be horrendous. It would be extremely difficult to prevent sterling appreciating in real terms and thus reducing some of the cost competitiveness of British industrial exports, although it would equally reduce internal inflationary pressures. Furthermore, if the underlying problem of the economy is the fundamental decline of British manufacturing industry, then it may do little to reverse it.

Yet, to use the North Sea benefits to expand domestic consumption in the hope of promoting investment is to risk letting loose forces for unproductive consumption which could quickly swallow-up any trade or balance of payments margin. If the basic imbalance of payments position is weak and if, as seems to be the case, export growth is still sluggish despite the exchange advantages and a recession in home demand, the actual balance of payments surplus induced by the North Sea may be only half or less of the notional figure produced on the basis that the economy without North Sea oil would achieve on current account. The production profiles on moderate assumptions show only a small surplus for exports over home consumption should the non-oil trade balance be in equilibrium. This surplus would only just be enough to pay off the debts directly attributable to borrowing against future oil revenues if the non-oil imbalance should rise to take account of the lack of oil imports. Past experience does not suggest that the non-oil trade surplus experienced in 1976 and early 1977 during a recession would hold for long once the economy picks up again.

Nor does past experience suggest that the capacity of central and local government to absorb sums once released from restriction has become less voracious, and is certainly more than enough to eat up any public sector revenue benefit of the North Sea.

Complicating this debate is the argument over exchange rates. A strong body within the Treasury and the Bank of England asserts that a basic objective over the medium-term must be to prevent sterling appreciating while the North Sea development encourages currency inflows and produces a balance of payments surplus. From this argument, an artificially high exchange rate can only serve to accelerate the decline of export industries and, when oil production begins to taper-off, leave the country with an overvalued currency and a weakened industry to produce the goods to pay for renewed oil imports. The most common moral tale used to reinforce this view is either the experience of Spain and South American gold in the sixteenth century or the more recent experience of the Netherlands, for whom gas exports already represent a benefit commensurate with the expected benefit of North Sea oil to the U.K. and which, it is alleged, has allowed the export revenues to sustain too high a rate of personal consumption and public expenditure, and too low a rate of investment.[10]

To prevent this happening in Britain, there has been a growing suggestion that exchange controls be eased to encourage an outward flow of funds, that possible measures on the Swiss and German example be introduced to discourage capital inflows and that a major proportion of the revenue and balance of payments benefits should be pre-empted for investment through industrial assistance and a special investment fund and for the early repayment of debt.

Countering this, however, there has been an equally strong argument that it is only by allowing sterling to appreciate that a "virtuous" circle can be created in which inflation at home is reduced, competitiveness is restored and growth will ensue. On this argument, sterling should be allowed to float freely on the exchanges, exchange controls should be phased out to counterbalance the inflation of money supply caused by the balance of payments surpluses and the growth in money supply at home should be kept under control while the revenues from the North Sea should be used to reduce taxation and restore incentive.

Whatever policy is adopted, of course, there will still be indirect benefits to the economy from the North Sea. If the current account balances are devoted to expanding foreign exchange reserves and

---

[10] The continued belief of officials in the need for a competitive exchange rate over the medium-term, contrasts, it must be said, with the short-term market and political pressures for allowing the rate to rise. In the summer of 1977, after six months of holding sterling's parity against the dollar and allowing it to depreciate against other countries, the rate was allowed to rise, partly because of Mr. Callaghan's personal conversion to the benefits for inflation and confidence in permitting this. There is evidence to suggest, however, that this was against the judgement of officials—a case once more of government opinions being overwhelmed by the unexpected force of the marketplace. For the Dutch experience, see Phillip's and Drew's *Market Review* of February 1977.

repayment of debt, there would be a follow-on impact through a lower public sector borrowing requirement and lower interest rates, benefitting both investment at home and increasing the current account surpluses. On the other course of expanding domestic consumption to the extent that the new balance of payments situation allows debt rescheduling, there would be bound to be some impact on higher domestic output and investment, whatever the import propensity. Using the tax revenues for increased public expenditure would lead to higher employment and higher consumption, just as lower taxation would do through activity in the private sector. Easing foreign exchange controls would have long-term benefits in foreign investment income to the country just as creating investment funds at home must have some long-term impact through increasing activity within Britain.

In so far as the argument is concerned about the efficiency with which North Sea benefits are used to promote long-term growth in productivity and investment, all evidence suggests the less intervention the better. The argument for deliberate intervention in the exchange markets to suppress sterling rests on the highly dubious grounds that falls in sterling bring anything but short-term gains. Indeed there is a strong argument that they increase rather than decrease the tendency of British industry to concentrate on the manufacture of goods of greatest price sensitivity and least value-added. The argument for state-run investment funds rests on equally dubious grounds that the civil service is more efficient in its choice of investments than is the market.

In so far as the argument is concerned with using the North Sea to achieve a dramatic breakthrough to sustained high-growth, the auguries are not good. None of the evidence suggests that the U.K.'s low growth is due to one simple factor such as lack of investment or high interest rates which could be resolved at the crack of the North Sea whip. The development of North Sea oil and gas provides time and a continuous boost to g.d.p. over a 20-year period. But it is not sufficiently large in its impact to alter one way or the other the long standing disputes as to whether British industry needs rebuilding behind import controls, whether it needs a fundamental improvement in labour productivity or any other basic economic reform.

Ultimately the benefit of the North sea rests on these more material factors, not the other way round. If the economy really was as vigorous as competitive economies on the Continent and was already well-prepared for growth without North Sea oil, then the impact of the new resource would be to accelerate British expansion on a very real scale.

As it is, any practical assessment must suggest that this is not the case. On reasonable assumptions, the combined direct and indirect benefits of the North Sea should be sufficient to raise the underlying growth rate in the U.K. by around 1 per cent per annum over the next ten years or so, enabling the U.K. to grow at perhaps 3 per cent a year. This would narrow the gap between the U.K. and its competitors, many of whom would be experiencing a less rapid growth since the imposition of high oil prices than they did on lower ones. But it would neither eliminate it, as U.K. growth rates might still be relatively low compared to others, nor would it enable the country to isolate itself from world economic pressures.

The opportunity that the North Sea gives is one of allowing a margin of time and a relaxation from balance of payments constraints in which to tackle the more basic problems of decline. The danger is that its very timing and the nature of its benefits over the immediate future will produce a euphoria and a competition for a share in its benefits which will make this task more difficult.

9 Siren or Saviour?

The North Sea now firmly stands as one of the most important and certainly the most unexpected economic developments to occur in Britain since the Second World War. For all the caution that has to be sounded over its ability to solve the country's long-standing economic problems of decline, the development of off-shore oil and gas has rapidly emerged in the last few years as a unique opportunity to look again at the U.K.'s economic prospects.

Already, the rapid rise in oil output during 1977 has served to revolutionise the balance of payments picture, provided a shot-in-the-arm for equity markets, helped to reduce interest rates and immeasurably strengthened sterling after the disastrous falls of the previous year. Over the next 15-20 years, it could have a continuing and profound effect on one of Britain's most persistent constraints on growth—that of its chronic balance of payments deficit. At a time when energy supplies and prices have posed serious questions as to the growth of the industrialised nations as a whole, it promises to make the country self-sufficient in energy, at least through the next decade and possibly into the 1990s. In a period when continued world recession has badly shaken political as well as public confidence in the national future, it has emerged as one of the few bright lights on the horizon.

Yet the development is also one that Britain can be grateful for rather than proud of and which, in many ways, it has done little to deserve and even less to manage well.

The story is certainly not one of unrelieved gloom. The initial decision to promote rapid exploration and development, for all the criticism of licensing terms since cast upon the early licence rounds, has at least enabled the country to get to the point where it is today —with a substantial production impetus underway, a major part of its territory explored and at least some concept of the resource and options at its disposal. Compared to the licensing terms and policies adopted in the initial rounds by other countries such as Denmark, Germany and Ireland, the first U.K. rounds could arguably be regarded as the outcome of unusual percipience and imagination by Government—and were at least a demonstration of initiative that succeeded in the aims as seen by officials at the time.

The initial decision to go for rapid gas industry conversion to natural gas, for all the short-term problems it has caused and the difficulties that the low price engendered in the supply position in the mid-seventies, was one of remarkable determination on the part of the gas industry and one which, in retrospect, appears to have been largely justified.

The efforts of individual companies to take advantage of the market for off-shore goods and services which the North Sea provided and forcefulness with which individual oil companies pursued ambitious plans for development and production, for all the delays, accident and confusion at the time, should not be underrated.

Yet the broad picture has been one in which the North Sea has tended to bring out the weaknesses rather than the strengths of the country and its institutions. From almost the beginning, and certainly from the time that oil was first tested in commercial flows, the story has been one in which government, politicians, industry and officials have understood too little and too late the implications of the exploration around them.

Later critics may have exaggerated the degree to which Government, with prodding, would have allowed tax loopholes to continue unclosed. But from the beginning North Sea policy has been marred persistently by the unspoken communion of interest between politicians and civil servants against any public debate of options wherever possible: by a marked tendency of Whitehall to rely almost exclusively on the advice of a few major companies such as Shell and BP; by the lack of real co-ordination between Departments, particularly the sponsoring Ministry for Power and the Treasury on tax questions and with the Department of Environment and Scottish Office on planning issues; and by the reluctance of the civil service either to build up outside expertise to understand and monitor new development or to allow any powers to be devolved on semi-autonomous bodies through which outside expertise could be brought in.

The result was a fourth round of licences which, by including an experimental auction, whetted the appetite but did nothing to tackle the question of tax; which geared up exploration at the cost of allocating most of the remaining potential acreage in the North Sea and much of the basin area to the West; and which created many of the radical policy actions which followed.

The resulting pendulum swing in Government attitudes in the last three years introduced a period of confused and ill-considered effort by politicians and officials to recover lost ground and make sense of vague political commitments, through a combination of tax measures, legislation to control production and depletion, the creation of a state corporation and negotiated participation in finds. These were never properly thought out as a whole and were introduced just as the North Sea programme was beginning to falter under the pressures of inflation and production delays.

Policies were pursued with persistent concentration on means rather than ends. Politicians persisted in an irrelevant game of denying that any problems of slow-down had emerged at all. The new Department of Energy was allowed to indulge the civil servant's inborn passion for controls which gave it the freedom to react to any circumstance at the expense of trying to understand just what those circumstances were. Far from learning from the mistakes of the past, the Government appeared to repeat them in its continual failure to sense the realities of Scottish nationalism and to create the institutions suitable to changing circumstances.

British industry, with some notable exceptions amongst individual companies, has been notoriously slow to respond to the opportunities provided by North Sea activity. If it has argued the difficulties of entering an area of new technology where the natural tendency of oil companies has been to rely on their traditional U.S. suppliers, then the Dutch, the French and the Norwegians (who have had none of the advantages of the early years of gas development which the U.K. has experienced), have proved themselves considerably more successful in overcoming them than their U.K. equivalents.

It has been argued that the problems of industrial and local response could have been eased by a slower pace of development and a less dramatic peak in ordering. This might have helped, but besides the economic implications for Britain today of slower oil development, the experience of the gas phase of development suggests that the reverse may be true: that only a dramatic push could have resulted in any interest at all being shown by U.K. companies.

It has also been argued that the Government itself should have done much more—as the French would have—to ensure a larger British response, but the experience of the Offshore Supplies Office in attempting to create consortium capacity and play a creative state role in industrial development is not one that gives much room for optimism either about the capacity of officials to create such entrepreneurial activities or about the ability of government subsidy or encouragement to induce growth when the fundamental initiative is not there in the first place.

The whole experience of building up capacity to construct platforms has been an even sharper lesson of the difficulties with which local communities and authorities have in the U.K. in coping with rapid new developments, in the lack of mobility of skills and labour in the country and in the way in which Government can turn its mind to a problem too late and come up with the wrong and expensive solution (in this case a radical expansion of capacity) just as the market has turned in an opposite direction. If business in Britain has been accused of being too conservative and too banking—orientated in its approach to new opportunities requiring heavy initial investment, the experience of the dramatic rise in ordering, and then the sudden falling off in demand, that the North Sea has undergone can only, regrettably, have tended to reinforce such conservatism.

That the country's response to the North Sea should in some ways be so unimpressive is not that surprising. If the besetting problems of the country are its declining manufacturing base, the unsuitability of traditional civil service training and promotion to its modern tasks, the adversary and unstable nature of its politics in recent times, poor economic management and a constant obsession with the balance of payments and exchange rates, it is hardly likely that North Sea policy and development would not have been influenced by the same factors rather than overcome them.

In the constant policy debate, not only over North Sea but over general industrial matters as well, whether the country should pursue the free-market path of Germany or the dirigiste path of France and Norway, it is often forgotten that the country has steadily lost its basic economic buoyancy and has lacked the necessary civil service qualities properly to follow either course.

A more interventionist policy on the North Sea might conceivably have been better from the start. It might have eased the problems of adjustment of industry and those of the regions to sudden surges in activity. It might have enabled Government to plan better its tax and depletion policy early on. It might have prevented some of the problems of strain that occurred during the 1972-5 period. But, judging from the experience of the 1967 White Paper on Energy (when the diametrically wrong conclusions about trends were reached) and the policy on platform construction sites, such a course could hardly have been carried out in practice without even worse blunders being suffered.

A free market solution might have been equally inappropriate, given the weakness of industry, the political hysteria that early policies have since aroused and the difficulties and strains which so much of the development, on and off-shore, encountered in the peak period of activity during 1972-4. Auctioning the licences would have done nothing to still the reaction at the time of the price explosion of 1974. Indeed it may well have only increased that reaction.

In the event, many of the problems which seemed so pressing at that time have been eased by the course of demand and production. The sudden fall in consumption growth which followed the "oil crisis" of 1973/4 and the delays in production programmes have done much to quieten Government enthusiasm for radical depletion control proposals. Yet, if the growth in demand had continued rising at pre-crisis rates and production programmes had then faltered, the cries would have been for faster, not slower, development. Equally, had demand slowed down and the production programmes kept to schedule, then the conservationist cry would have been all the greater.

As it is, the fall in the rate of growth in demand for oil has been more than sufficient to compensate for the delays and the slowing-down in production profiles—illustrating yet again the point that events take their own course rarely in line with the projections of the time.

Provided nothing goes seriously awry, Britain is now in the happy position of being able to look forward to self-sufficiency in energy over the next ten years at a time when the rest of the world is still trying to cope with the implications of the 1973/4 crisis, as well as a balance of trade and monetary boost of very considerable proportions just as the country was in great difficulties.

It can control depletion rates or accelerate development, repay debt or use the benefits to expand consumption, cut taxes or maintain public expenditure, and devalue or revalue the currency—options which, in theory at least, are almost unprecedented since the war and which most other European countries would give much to possess.

But it is precisely because recent events appear to have eased the problems of delay, and recent trends in balance of payments and

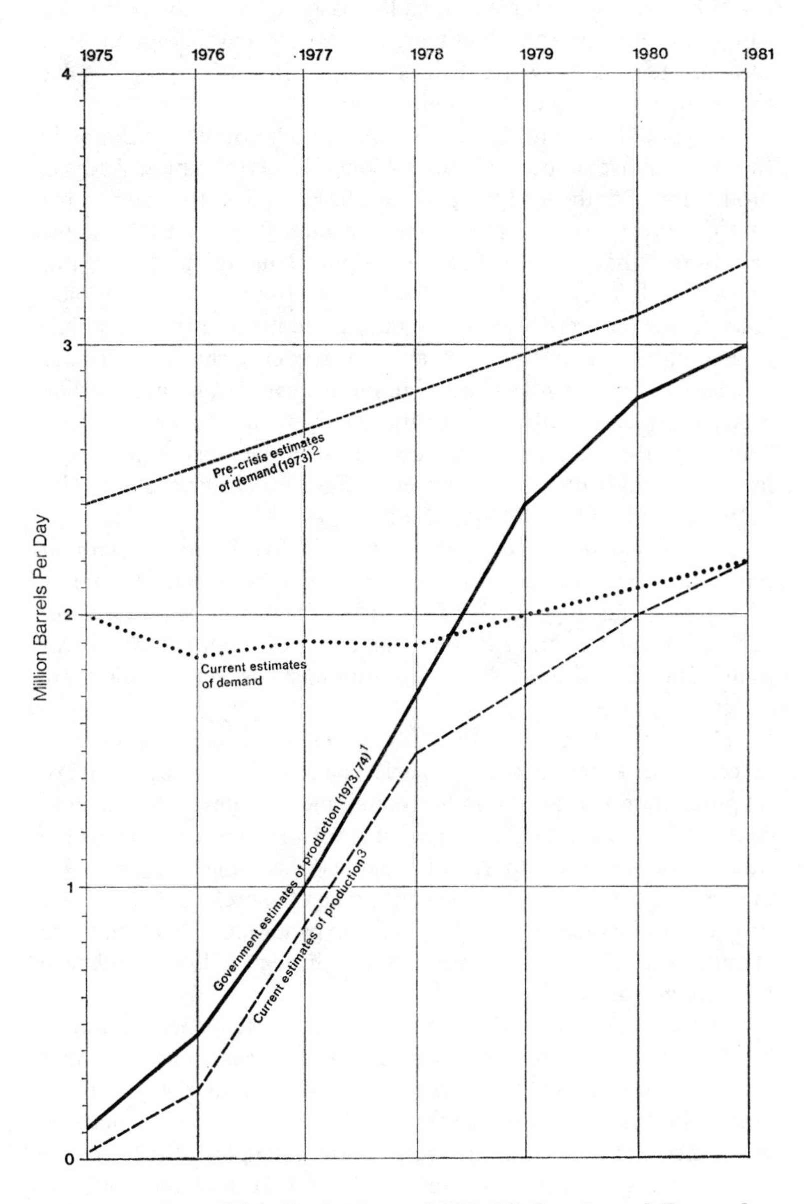

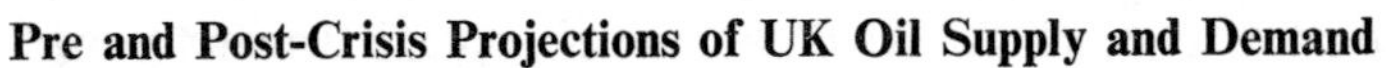
Pre and Post-Crisis Projections of UK Oil Supply and Demand

investment appear to have created the basis on which the North Sea can perform its miracles, that there is a danger that the options may seem greater than they are. By itself, it does little or nothing to solve the country's energy or economic problems.

As an additional resource it is valuable but not overwhelming in the context of the country's total economic performance. At best, production over the next ten years will be equivalent to around 6 per cent of current g.n.p., giving a modest annual boost to economic growth rates but not enough to alter significantly the pattern of low growth experienced before the oil crisis. If the current account balance now being sought is maintained and if the growth of public expenditure continues to be restrained, the Government will have choices in repayment of debt, domestic expansion and sterling exchange valuation. But the country has had balances and restraint before—at the beginning of the decade—and then lost them; and it has had periods of high investment before which have not significantly altered underlying growth rates.

In notional terms of what life would have been like without North Sea, the oil and gas flows may be very important. In terms of the personal experience of Britons—whether it will be easier to find jobs and whether they will be better off than before oil was found and the oil crisis blew up—optimism is very much more difficult to express.

The attractive timing of the development of the North Sea may indeed present the greatest problems. The most important impact of oil production will not be in ten years time, despite the tendency to consider it over the medium term, but over the next few years as the trade impact builds up rapidly and as the monetary flows hit the economy. Yet this is the very time when the pressures on current policies of income restraint, public expenditure curbs and the maintenance of export competitiveness through a lower exchange rate, are greatest.

Nor do the country's energy problems suddenly disappear because of the presence of North Sea oil and gas. It may be that they can form a long-term resource to the end of the century if new basin discoveries are brought in. But it is conceivable that the newer licensed areas off the west coasts could have little if any commercial quantities of oil or gas. It may be that there will be room for net exports of oil in the middle-eighties if demand growth is relatively low and additional fields are brought in continuously. It could equally be that there will be a net deficit of oil in the eighties if demand growth accelerates because of the impact of the North Sea on economic growth and if new discoveries are not made sufficiently rapidly.[1]

One of the major legacies of the last two years' pause in development is that the period has left the country with a feeling of confidence about ultimate reserves and production but not the practical assurance of those benefits, let alone the assurance that more oil will be discovered off the west coasts.

But a crisis in the sense that the Government and economists talk of—a dramatic drawing together of the lines of demand and supply until they cross and the world is short of energy—is most unlikely. If the pressures do arise, the reaction will almost certainly be a sudden and dramatic rise in oil prices and a diversion of investment and effort into the energy field by the consumers as the producers respond to the picture well in advance of the critical point. This in turn will bring its own ramifications on economic growth, reduced energy consumption and the development of alternatives. The question is rather at what cost alternative sources can be developed and what restraints on economic growth the energy question will place.

In these circumstances, it is quite right that a Government should worry about investing the benefits of one fuel, oil, in the development of alternatives and to consider its depletion options. But the lesson of the last "crisis" was quite clearly that the implications of high oil prices on the economy as a whole and the implications of a recession in trade on every country, with or without energy resources of its own, cannot be ignored. With this in mind it is little less than grossly irresponsible to talk, as officials as well as Ministers in the Department of Energy do, of Britain benefitting from a rise in prices or a supply crisis necessitating tight nationalistic control of supply. As Iran and other producers have found after the last crisis, no country can divorce itself from the general condition of

---

[1] As in other countries, the connection between higher growth rates and higher oil usage tends to be forgotten. If the North Sea really enables the U.K. to grow at a rate of 3-5 per cent through the next ten years, as some commentators suggest, then oil demand would almost certainly shoot up to over 3m. barrels per day in 1980 and 3·5-4m. barrels per day by 1985, thus exceeding the more moderate assumptions of supply by the early to mid-eighties and forcing a rapid acceleration in the development programme. It is this persistent and concealed energy constraint on economic growth which lies at the heart of the energy problem for all the developed world and which helps make the future so difficult to read.

world trade. This must be even more so for a country such as Britain, for whom the North Sea represents only a small proportion of g.d.p. and only a fraction of total employment.

The approach being adopted by Government and the institutional framework developed to answer these questions is hardly reassuring. If the lesson of the past is that Britain has consistently reacted too late to changing circumstances and that Government and critics have spent too much time in excessive niggling over means rather than ends, and prejudices rather than possibilities, there is little sign that the lessons have been learned.

As in the early years of the formation of North Sea policy, when decisions were made by discreet compromises between interested institutions on unquestioned assumptions about balance of payments and British interest, so at present the debate takes place behind closed doors on a new and unquestioned set of assumptions—that there will be an energy gap in the 1990s if not the late eighties, that a high exchange rate will damage the manufacturing industry, that the pace of development and depletion can and should be controlled, that investment should be directed to industry, that Britain should adopt a nationalistic approach to the question of oil prices and oil supplies and that increasing consumption is *per se* undesirable.

The weight of history would suggest quite the opposite—that the future is a great deal more unpredictable than these views would assume and that the cause and effect in economic growth is too little understood to provide simple answers.

On the North Sea and the broader front, it may be right to suggest that, on current trends, the world is heading once more for a tight supply situation with renewed dependence on the Middle East and a lack of immediate alternatives in nuclear or other energy forms. Certainly the developments—or lack of them—over the last few years since the 1973 crisis would indicate that this is true.

It would also seem far from wise to assume simple answers to the question of depletion control. If there is a steady rise in real prices for energy until the end of the century, it may be sensible to conserve resources—although such a pattern of prices would tend to have this effect on company investment in any case. If there is a sudden and dramatic price rise in the early to mid-eighties in response to a picture appearing on the horizon, then the question of conservation must depend on what view is taken on consumer reaction to this price rise throughout the industrialised West—in the form of technology, alternative supplies and conservation in use—

and what effects this will have on prices and supply in the 1990s. For Britain, the question of depletion must also depend on the view of the likely resources to be found all around its shores, and particularly in the unexplored areas.

The means of ensuring a flexible response to these uncertainties is less likely to lie in piling ever more control mechanisms on the development, giving officials freedom to intervene at will, than in continuing to promote exploration and development while maintaining some restricted control on production. Knowledge in geology is best acquired through competition and this in turn is best maintained by ensuring a counterweight to the large international companies—whose investment is controlled by their international needs (no bad thing in itself)—in the presence of smaller, high-risk-taking companies. Development could be encouraged through tax incentives. On the broader energy front, meanwhile, it would seem best to maintain co-operation with competitor countries, whose greater need for oil substitutes could be expected to induce more resource allocation in this direction.

These aims are not inconsistent with the publicly declared policy of the Government. But its approach in practice would appear to be going in a different direction. By establishing a separate Department of Energy with wide-ranging legislative controls, it has encouraged an attitude of mind behind policy-making which is innately limited in its understanding of the broader economic and international environment in which oil plays a part, which tends towards tinkering as a justification of existence, and which approaches energy problems as a chess board on which the different fuels can be moved around to form a "correct" pattern rather than creating maximum flexibility of interchange at the margin.

In the Off-shore Supplies Office, the Government has an agency which, by the nature of its political terms of reference, is almost bound to concentrate on maximum import substitution (the old cry from the beginnings of the North Sea) rather than the points at which U.K. technology and capital have the greatest chance of international success. In its tax system, the country has a charge that discourages successful companies from re-investing profits in further developments, discourages marginal investment by the new prospector and, by offering over-generous relief in the early years with the aim of achieving a higher take in later years, could well raise again considerable political criticism when the size of the cash flow on the early major oil fields becomes apparent.

In the British National Oil Corporation it has created a strange agency whose development is difficult to read. The case for a state oil company, as a counterbalance to the weight of the oil companies, as a means of direct experience for the Government and as an instrument for investment which the country may want, but the oil industry would be unwilling to undertake, is a strong one.

However, the case for negotiated participation in all commercial finds using a state corporation as the holding agency is less clear. The experience of Statoil in Norway, ENI in Italy, and Elf-Aquitaine in France, is that the state oil corporations very quickly take on ambitions of their own that are in direct contradiction with the Government's interests and fall too easily in line with those of the major companies. Participation in the British case can only increase this tendency and one's fear is that, far from encouraging exploration and development in the North Sea and adding an extra element of investment, the natural self-interest of BNOC will be to insist on the licence allocations and the programmes which would otherwise be carried out just as efficiently by the independent oil companies, and that it will develop its own monopolistic tendencies.

The need for the major oil companies is a straightforward one—they can carry out their work more efficiently than other bodies, and thus leave national resources for more productive tasks. The reason for additional action is that, in the end, the interests of the companies are not necessarily those of the nation under all circumstances, so that it is wise to have both some direct supervision and some countervailing force. It is hard to see BNOC carrying out this function in practice when so many of its interests will tend to be the same as those of the oil companies—particularly at a time when the independent companies are being squeezed out of the action. Still less is it easy to see the need for control of half the oil through participation when BNOC will have no direct use for this product unless there is a state of emergency, in which case the right already exists of residual state intervention through legislation.

None of this need prove disastrous. There is sufficient impetus already underway, and a sufficient variety of companies, to ensure continued exploration and development. The post-war British political obsession for seeking change through reform of institutions is to some extent mitigated by the ineffectiveness of those institutions. But it does mean, as in the earlier years of development, that unspoken policy decisions are reached on the need for conservation, the development of coal, the necessity of control and the role of the independents which are never tested in public debate; which are arrived at behind the scenes and whose alternatives are never really considered.

The same could be said of the current approach within Government to the economic policy questions raised by North Sea oil. Despite the overriding importance of the development, and in strong contrast to the Norwegians, whose regular reports by the Departments of Industry and Finance are a model of open government, there has still been no real presentation of alternative policies by Government and remarkably little publication of its calculations and approach. Instead, officials and politicians have reacted as much in fear as in enthusiasm for the potential opened up; alternatively claiming too much for its benefits and regarding them as a dangerous promoter of evil living and lack of discipline. Assumptions about the need to keep sterling "competitive", to give priority to the repayment of debt, to encourage manufacturing investment through the development of special funds as well as judgements from the experience of the Norwegians and the Dutch, have all crept in to the point where they are close to becoming Government policy without anyone realising it—the classic collusion between civil servants and politicians to avoid public debate.

Yet the evidence to support these assumptions is a debatable one. Intervention in the exchange markets deliberately to force down the value of sterling has not, on the evidence of the disastrous 1976 experience, been particularly successful, nor does the experience of previous efforts to restrain home demand and promote export growth through devaluation suggest that the benefits are anything but short-term. If U.K. costs consistently rise at a much higher rate than those of its competitors, then sterling would probably depreciate over the longer-term even with North Sea oil. Allowing the North Sea benefits to maintain sterling at a higher level could be said to have at least an equal chance of reducing domestic inflationary expectations and thereby promoting growth.

The experience of the Norwegians is not directly comparable, since oil and gas there are of infinitely larger magnitude relative to the size of the economy than in the U.K. Even there, the recent experience of recession has raised questions about the validity of the restrictive approach adopted in 1973, since the non-oil areas of the economy are suffering more than expected and are no longer in competition with oil for jobs and resources in the ways predicted. The Dutch experience of Groningen gas is more directly comparable to the U.K. situation in relative size of impact. There is a strong argument that, as with Britain, there was a natural collusion between the Finance Ministry and the oil companies to seek rapid exploitation and to maximise exports, with damaging consequences over the longer term. By comparison the U.K. does not have the opportunity for oil export which the Netherlands, with its smaller internal needs, had with gas.[2]

If the Dutch really have experienced declining industrial investment and rising unemployment to an unusual degree over the last few years (as, indeed, have all developed countries), it could be argued that this is less the result of an overvalued currency from gas exports than the domestic combination of high corporate tax, indexed wages and high personal consumption which have preempted the benefits of the gas. As a small country, the Netherlands, with or without gas, was likely to have concentrated on improving the quality of its investment rather than production expansion and employment. In this they have not been unsuccessful.

The evidence on the broader question as to how to use North Sea benefits for generating investment suggests that demand rather than interest or subsidies promotes investment. Growth is as dependent upon psychological and social factors (or simply general optimism about the future) as it is on any mechanical calculation of returns, profits or the availability of low-cost finance.

From this viewpoint, what is encouraging about the North Sea is that it may create a psychological momentum of hope, confidence and subsequent expansionary investment. Just as important, it gives for

---

[2] Surprisingly little has been written in the U.K. about the Dutch experience, although it seems to form the basis of a number of judgements in the Treasury. Estimates of the balance of payments and revenue benefit of Dutch gas and the co-incidental fall in investment have been made by Graham Bishop in Phillips and Drew's *Market Review,* February 1977—although this does not establish any direct relationship between gas production, appreciating exchange rates and investment decline. The Dutch Government, however, appear to be taking the exchange rate problem seriously now. So are the Norwegians who, despite North Sea oil and gas, devalued their currency together with other Scandinavian countries in the summer of 1977. Their fears that traditional Norwegian industry could become uncompetitive under the exchange rate, employment and inflationary pressures of off-shore development, has encouraged this attempt both to try to keep their exchange rate in line with other Scandinavian countries and to spend heavily to subsidise industry. It could be argued, however, that the Norwegian combination of restricting off-shore development while attempting to sustain growth rates through borrowing and public expenditure has compounded the mistake and has left them in a weaker position to cope with the recession with less opportunity for structural change than would otherwise have been the case.

almost the first time since the war the opportunity for Governments to follow a consistent policy towards demand expansion, within the limits that the balance of payments allows, and removes some of the policy and psychological obstacles of balance of payments deficits and dramatic sterling movements which have so bedevilled previous efforts to achieve this consistency.

The danger is that policies adopted may produce the opposite tension. Intervention in the exchange markets, deliberate constraints imposed through accelerated repayment of debt, direction of revenues to industrial investment, and the political squabble over its handling, could all tend to make policy more, not less, volatile.

Any deliberate attempt to postpone the benefits of the North Sea by pre-empting them for the repayment of debt and for Government investment funds is all too likely to be subsumed as unions move to pre-empt them in the form of higher wages. So long as there is no public acceptance of how the revenues from oil and gas, both direct and indirect, should be used, the chances are that the sense of relief that the North Sea will promote in society will encourage a scramble for those resources in calls for lower taxes, higher public expenditure and higher wages which will overwhelm the relatively modest size of the benefits.

The question of tax revenues remains overcast by the very real questions as to how far the Scots will demand a major share. At the moment, under the present constitution, Scotland stands to experience a decline in its traditional high-employment industries which will more than outweigh the direct employment and investment it stands to gain from the North Sea. For all the present tendency to push this issue to the background, it seems inconceivable that the Scottish nation will stand aside and let this happen, or that they will be satisfied with greater regional investment assistance through special funds or agencies. Only a direct and visible share in the revenues themselves—certainly the royalties and probably a share in the petroleum revenue tax as well—appears likely to smooth the resulting tensions. Whatever happens, a discussion of the potential benefits of the North Sea would seem peculiarly unrealistic without a recognition of this factor.

The idea of an investment fund for industry and the regions—much beloved by Ministers at present—would seem an equally dubious response to the options presented by North Sea. It has the obvious attraction of seeming to put aside funds for longer-term investment in the manufacturing sector. It could be presented as a means of answering the particular needs of Scotland and the declining regions. However, it begs all the questions of whether it is investment *per se* which has been lacking in Britain. The fund would have to be worth several billions of pounds if it was to mean much, which exposes the obvious argument as to whether a Government-directed fund is the most effective means of answering the problems of growth which it would set out to tackle. The experience of the last few years is that Governments, whatever their intentions, inevitably bow to particular political pressures for job preservation in declining industries, for aid to be directed to high unemployment regions and for money to be spent in rescue operations. It is difficult to believe that an initiative so politically sensitive as a North Sea Fund would prove any different.

The fear aroused by the Government's belated efforts to tackle the North Sea economic debate is that Ministers and officials will once again present a number of limited options as if they were the only alternatives reflecting the real uncertainties. The basic assumptions about energy choices, rates of output, institutions for control, the international environment, the economic policy objectives, exchange rate implications and profit and monetary flow effects will remain unstated. The implicit decisions on policy which have already been taken, through default as much as intention, will be taken for granted and the North Sea will be treated as a defined pot of gold that can be spent in this direction or that without any regard to the complexity and the unknown factors about its impact in the market-place.

Fortunately, the impetus of North Sea developments is probably now strong enough to survive even the most disastrous of policies and still have beneficial effects on the economy. Even if the entire balance of payments benefit was lost in higher consumption and imports and even if all the tax revenues were dissipated in unrestrained public expenditure, it would still have some effect in promoting additional investment and jobs. The impact of higher corporate sector profits and the monetary flows associated with oil production must be felt in the stock market, in finance and in capital expenditure by companies. The effect of foreign currency inflows and a stronger sterling exchange rate must be beneficial on internal inflation and the general atmosphere of confidence.

The magnitude of North Sea benefits are certainly too small to meet all the competing claims which may be made upon them. The North Sea cannot be expected to provide a panacea for all the problems that the British economy has experienced in the last two decades. But, in estimating these benefits, the most obvious point may simply be that, as a new resource, we still understand too little about its potential size to make easy judgements on its exploitation and too little about its impact on the economy to judge the true implications of the resultant development on British growth. Still less do we understand enough of the broader environment of energy supply and demand, growth in world trade and the future course of industrial expansion in the western economies to make simple policy decisions.

The central importance of the North Sea to Britain, may indeed, lie less in the calculations of revenue and balance of payments effects than in its timing. It has finally started to flow at a time when the era of cheap energy seems to have been shattered, at least for the next decade and more, by the crisis of 1973/4. Whether there will be a real crisis of supply in the next decade or not—and there is reason enough to doubt it—the presence of substantial indigenous supplies of oil and gas in an era of high energy import costs in the world must bring long-term benefits, if for no other reason than that it eases this constraint on growth.

In the same way, North Sea oil has finally broken into the British consciousness just as the country and the industrialised world is still shuffling out of a recession, which raises fundamental doubts over long-term growth rates of the West. The opportunity that the North Sea gives for governments to follow more consistently expansionary and stable economic policies than before; the effect that it could have on interest rates and revenues; and, just as important, the changes it may bring to business confidence and national optimism may all have much more far reaching implications than narrow economic calculations allow for.

The danger is that oil is now coming precisely at the moment when the pressures of high unemployment, wage tensions and political uncertainty are strongest. Just as it could ease the pressures and open the way to greater optimism and economic stability, so could it also intensify the pressures by arousing expectations and short-term policy reactions that could soon overwhelm its benefits.

Appendices

Appendix I

Map of UK Continental Shelf licensing rounds

Appendix II

Map of sedimentary basins, UK Continental Shelf

Appendix III
Map of UK Continental Shelf

Index

Page numbers in italic refer to graphs.
Page numbers with suffix n refer to footnotes.

A

B

C

D

E

F

G

H

I

J

K

L

M

N

O

P

R

S

T

U

V

W

Z